Moscow's Final Solution: The Genocide of the German-Russian Volga Colonies

DARREL PHILIP KAISER

Published August 2007
Darrel P. Kaiser

Darrel Kaiser Books
www.DarrelKaiserBooks.com
email:Dar-Bet@att.net

Second Printing

ISBN 978-0-6151-5780-1

The Author

Darrel P. Kaiser has been researching the development of the Germanic peoples and his ancestors for over 10 years. While living in Bavaria and Germany for over two years, he "walked the lanes" and did on-site research in the villages of his ancestors.

He has also been professionally troubleshooting electrical, electronic, and mechanical components and systems for the US Government for the last 37 years. During those years, Darrel also trained with *PFAFF* in Germany and *BERNINA* USA in the art of professional sewing machine repair, and continues repair and restoration even today.

After all those years of troubleshooting and repair, he turned to teaching at a Government University and writing technical books. Out of his research came his first book on Germanic History and Genealogy, "*Origins and Ancestors Families Karle & Kaiser of the German-Russian Volga Colonies.*"

Darrel has also written and published numerous other books on German and Russian History, Politics, Religion, and Ancestry; a book on the Watercolor quilts of Betty Kaiser, a book on basic electrical troubleshooting, a book on sewing machine troubleshooting, two books on the SINGER 221 *Featherweight*, and two books on the

STANDARD *Sewhandy* and GE *MODEL A* sewing machines. This book's final pages show all the titles.

For more on his research into German and Russian History and Genealogy, visit his website at
www.Volga-Germans.com

For more on his books on Troubleshooting, visit his website at
www.BasicTroubleshooting.com

For more on his books about Sewing Machines, visit his website at
www.SewingMachineTech.com

For more on his books about the STANDARD *Sewhandy* and GE *MODEL A* sewing machines, visit his website at
www.SewhandySewingMachines.com

For more information on all of his books, visit his website at
www.DarrelKaiserBooks.com

Preface

By 1860, the Russian Governments and Russian People did not want the German-Russians in Russia. They tried everything to rid their Russia of this "German" problem, but finally had to resort to Murder, Rape, and Deportation to accomplish their goal.

There is a word for this type of treatment against a People – GENOCIDE.

If you look at just one event, it appears that the German-Russians were just unlucky. If you look at "the big picture" over a hundred years, a pattern becomes evident.

This book covers that pattern and includes the famines caused by Nature and the Government policies that made the famines one hundred times worse. It includes the discriminatory Laws that the Russian Governments passed to drive the German-Russians out.

It documents the events and actions that led up to the deportation of the German-Russians from the Volga Colonies, and the horrible conditions they endured as they attempted to survive in Siberia and other areas, as "less than human beings."

Also discussed is the retraction of charges by the Krushchev and the Soviet Government leading to the German-Russians release from their exile, and the eventual realization that they are a "People" with no homeland.

This book is one in a series on the History, Religion, Politics, and Ancestry of the German-Russians of the Volga Colonies. Among the others are:

"Origin & Ancestors Families Karle & Kaiser of the German-Russian Volga Colonies"

"Religions of Germany and the German-Russian Volga Colonies"

"The Bad and Downright Ugly of the German-Russian Volga Colonies"

"Emigration To and From the German-Russian Volga Colonies"

I have also written and published other books on a variety of topics including basic electrical troubleshooting, watercolor quilts, sewing machine repair, and the STANDARD Sewhandy and SINGER Featherweight sewing machines.

For more information about all my books, please visit my websites at

www.DarrelKaiserBooks.com
www.Volga-Germans.com

Your comments and/or submissions to improve the value of this book will always be appreciated. Discussions as to the validity of my theories and assumptions are welcome.

Submission of copies of photographs or documents that are applicable to the subject is encouraged, and credit will be given in the next edition. Feel free to contact me by email at Dar-Bet@att.net .

I sincerely hope you find this book interesting and educational! I did.

Table of Contents

Preface

Chapter 1: Introduction to Genocide   1

Chapter 2: The Downward Trend   3

      Russian Paranoia   7

Chapter 3: The Russian Famine 1891 -1892   9

Chapter 4: World War I   17

Chapter 5: Lenin   23

      Rebellion in Warenburg   27

Chapter 6: Another Famine Arrives   37

Chapter 7: Volga Relief Society   49

Chapter 8: Stalin Assumes Power   57

Chapter 9: Famine Again   59

Chapter 10: Russian (Stalin) Paranoia   65

Chapter 11: Deported to Die   *67*

Chapter 12: Did the World Even Care?   *79*

Chapter 13: Reversal of Deportations   *89*

Summary   *95*

Bibliography   *97*

End Notes   *107*

Chapter 1
Introduction to Genocide

There are some that believe that what happened to the German-Russians of the Volga Colonies was not Genocide. They believe that it was just an unfortunate series of unrelated occurrences for an unlucky people in one particular location.

I suppose this could be true, but I do not believe it. The historical records show a clear trend of prejudicial and discriminatory treatment starting with the Russian Tsarist Governments.

This treatment continued and dramatically increased after the Communists eventually seized power. It was directed at all Germans in Russia, but the German-Russians of the Volga Colonies seem to suffer the worst. Maybe it was not the Governments, but the Russian people themselves punishing another group for their own centuries of misfortune.

Genocide is defined as the deliberate and systematic destruction of a racial, political, or cultural group.[1] It is defined by the Convention on the Prevention and Punishment of the Crime of Genocide (CPPCG) Article 2 with the following statement, "any of the following acts committed with intent to destroy, in whole or in part, a national, ethnic, racial or religious group, as such: Killing members of the group; Causing serious bodily or mental harm to members of the group; Deliberately inflicting on the group conditions of life calculated to bring about its physical destruction in whole or in part; Imposing measures intended to prevent births within the group; and forcibly transferring children of the group to another group."[2]

Some may argue that the famines caused by the Russian Governments were not Genocide, as they were not directed specifically against the German-Russians of the Volga Colonies, they also inflicted terrible horrors on the Ukrainians and even their own Russian people. My view is that the Russian Government pursued multiple atrocities and genocides at the same time.

In any case, another word may be more accurate. Democide is defined as "the murder of any person or people by a government, including genocide, politicide, and mass murder". Government-sponsored killings for political reasons would be democide.

Democide would include deaths arising from "intentionally or knowingly reckless and depraved disregard for life"; or mass starvations.[3] Other historians have included the Great Purges carried out by Stalin as an example of Democide since it was an action against all groups in Russia.

This book will show that both the Famines, the forced deportation of the German-Russians of the Volga Colonies, and the eradication of any trace of their former presence and culture were both Genocide and Democide.

Where and when did it all start? That is *the rest of the story.*"

Chapter 2
The Downward Trend

Tsarina Catherine the Great spent a great amount of time and money convincing her German people to leave their homeland and to settle in Russia. One would think that the succeeding Tsars would value them as an asset, but one would be wrong.

The reality was that the Volga German-Russians had outlived the Tsarina's need to use her former countrymen (and my ancestors) as a human barrier to keep out the unwanted, and to extend her power. The area was now fairly civilized, and now even more than before, the Germans were both unwelcome and expendable.

By the mid 1800's, Russia was a country in deep trouble. It was almost hopelessly behind the development of other European States. Fundamental reforms were inevitable and Tsar Alexander II introduced reforms in 1861. However, he did not eliminate the oppressive land poverty of most farmers in Russia since the aristocrats' feudal large-landed property could not be touched.[4]

When Tsar Alexander II emancipated all the Russian serfs, they immediately had equal status with our German ancestors. This ended our ancestors "privileged status" that was granted by Catherine the Great.

Ten years later in 1871, the Volga Colonies right to self-government ended with the nullification of the colonial law that granted it.

Tsar Alexander II [5]

Remember the "no military service" promise that the Recruiters gave to the Germans back in Germany 100 years earlier. Russian Military service requirements were reformed on January 1, 1874 by the "law for the introduction of the general compulsory military service". The modernization of the Russian army required this mandatory or draft military duty.

All German-Russian men of 21 years now had six years active military service to carry out, and nine years reserve time. Even today, pictures of young Germans in Russian uniforms are found among our ancestral photographs. [6]

Mr. John Bitter (left) from Laube and Mr. Michael Leisle in soldier uniforms in Russian Army in 1907.

Mr. Philip Arndt (center) from Warenburg - Russian Army - Taken 1894.

Soldiers in Russian Army
From left; A Russian;
Rev. J. C. Bitter,
Mr. Carl P. Christian.

11   Fred Nielsen of Stahl - In Russian Navy 1904.

It is reported that after the first young colonial men were drafted into the army, stories of their poor treatment spread along the Volga. This poor treatment included flogging for even the smallest discretions.[7] Subsequently, thousands of twenty-year-old boys quickly decided to leave the country.[8]

For many, this meant the loss of the last of the Tsarina Catherine the Great privileges. In the poem below, "the communist manifesto," the colonists' disgust comes thru:

"We left our native country
And pulled into the Russian country,
The Russians were very much beneidt us,
And because we were so long released,
Thus Sie's brought there with cunning,
That we no more should not be Kolonist.

Egg Kolonisten are not we more
And must carry the rifle.
What by the envy happens nevertheless?
One the communist manifesto vernicht't
Originate from the German Reich,
Now we are alike to the Russians." [9]

The German-Russians religious freedom was also under attack, with laws now in effect prohibiting their ownership of land unless they converted to the Orthodox faith.[10]

In 1892, Alexander III outlawed land acquisition by non-Orthodox citizens in the west. To land-starved colonists who had helped found many new colonies and who had plans to start more, this policy seemed to aim directly at their freedom of religion which Catherine had also guaranteed.[11]

An anti-German feeling was building across the steppes and the colonists felt it. The Volga German-Russian colonists only had two choices, one was to stay and accept the changes, or two was to leave.

Colonists slowly began to emigrate to America, Canada, Brazil, and Argentina. Between 1874 and 1890, it is estimated that 30,000 Germans left Russia for the new freedoms of the Americas.[12]

Russian Paranoia

Even as the German Colonists were leaving Russia, the Russian public was becoming increasingly discriminatory and paranoid. There was much discussion among the Russians arguing whether the original migration had been a benefit to Russia. Some felt that it was of no long-term benefit, while others felt that the Catherine the Great program had been beneficial to the country. Russian newspapers ran complete analysis of how the German Kolonisten had fulfilled their duties in comparison to their Russian neighbors.

Eventually, the rational discussions were replaced with the emotional nationalistic feelings of the Russian public. This became even worse after the German Reich gained power in 1871 and moved towards it foreign policy of expansion. In the discussion around the "German question," the increasing property holdings of the German Kolonisten played an important role. The Russian feeling was that the Germans (especially wealthy Germans) were not to be trusted, and that included the German-Russians that had been living off the bounty of Mother Russia for 100 years.

Because of nationalistic propaganda, the Russians feared a "peaceful conquest." The Russian population feared an expansion of Germany into the Russian-German colonies.[13]

This growing resentment and distrust of the German-Russians would become an obsession in the years to come. After all, these German-Russians would never be Russians no matter how long they lived there... They were still just Germans with first loyalty to Berlin.

Chapter 3
The Russian Famine 1891-1892

In 1891 thru 1892, a famine hit Russia. This was not the first famine in Russia. The Nikonian Chronicle, written between 1127 and 1303, listed eleven famine years in Russia during that time. Russian Tsar Alexander I was the first Russian Monarch to attempt to create a comprehensive famine relief system in 1822. Tsar Nicholas I established a network of granaries and changed the system in 1834. The idea was that the peasants should stock up in good years and then empty out during a crop failure. While this theory looked good on paper, in practice it was a complete failure. Even in the best years the peasants were too poor to contribute, and where the granaries actually existed they were usually empty. History also records a famine in the year 1873. This is when Leo Tolstoy became aware of the seriousness of a famine in Samara when he was visiting his estate there.

The famine of 1891-1892 was particularly bad. It affected the population of an area of around 900,000 square miles in the Volga and central agricultural areas. At times these were the most fertile and productive parts of Russia. They included the provinces of Nizhni-Novgorod, Riazan, Tula, Kazan, Simbirsk, Saratov, Penza, Samara and Tambov.

The famine came about partially because of a recent past of poor harvests (6 of the last 12 years). Between the years of 1879 and 1889, six of the years saw poor harvests. These harvests had been negatively affected by both natural problems and by man-made circumstances (drought, population growth, poor growing seasons, and soil erosion).

The dry autumn of 1891 delayed the seeding of the fields. The winter began early and was more severe than usual, with only light snowfall. Heavy snow usually protects the seedlings from the cold. Normally, melting snow and ice would cause spring floods of the Volga. The floodwaters would spread over the plains whose grass was used as fodder for the animals. However, this year the small amount of snow only caused the ground to freeze.

AREA OF FAMINE IN RUSSIA 1891 - 1892

14

The freezing killed the young plants because the delayed seeding and late planting did not give new plants enough time to take root. The bad weather eliminated the main source of feed for the animals. The animal's health was crucial to the peasants because they provided the power needed to plow the fields. The cold weather lasted until mid-April. The summer of 1892 was extremely hot and dry with five rainless months. This resulted in the smallest total grain harvest for European Russia in a decade.

The famine was at its worst in Ukraine and the Volga region. Local authorities were hesitant to report the famine, as they would look bad. The problem was covered up while the people starved. When the central government did learn of the famine, it was also reluctant to acknowledge it since they would also look bad. Also, there was the theory that the central government directed movement of farmers from small plots to large farms was a major contributing factor to the famine's outbreak. Even after the famine was known, the government continued exporting food products from the famine area to overseas markets. This caused more people to starve. Of course, it also brought money into the central government treasury.

Count Leo Tolstoy was a vocal critic of the government. He blamed it for its policies regarding the famine, while also criticizing the relief efforts implemented by the state. He felt the government had not understood the true causes of the famine and they did not know what was really going on in the famine area. He also believed they were mishandling the relief efforts.

Tolstoy wanted the government to collect exact statistics by sending officials into the villages to compile the data needed for wise and efficient aid.[15] Tolstoy also claimed that the government provided no help for laborers who were able to work, and for those with horses or cattle. He reported that large quantities of grain were either stolen or allowed to spoil, thus wasting precious food and money.

Tolstoy suggested the construction of large-scale public works, the regulation of grain, and forbidding the hoarding of flour. He also supported the opening of sufficient free eating-houses in famine villages, along with the organization of all available voluntary forces in national relief work. The Russian Government in St. Petersburg ignored his suggestions.

Leo Tolstoy

16

Not satisfied with this, Tolstoy left Yasnaya Polyana and went to his estate in the Dankovsky district. There, he gathered information on the needs of each family and individual. He set up eating rooms of his own that provided two meals a day and a supply of wood for fuel during the winter in exchange for work. For those unable to work and most needy, it was free.

At the same time, his wife was collecting donations for his work in Moscow. Tolstoy and his wife opened soup booths in twenty-two villages, and set up corn and clothing stores for those suffering.[17] Tolstoy also made sure that horses and work materials were supplied to the people in order to help them make their own clothes and shoes. He bought the surplus goods at full price and distributed them among the poorest people. To prevent a repetition of the famine, he provided seed and replaced horses so the peasants would be able to plant and prepare for the next harvest.[18] He remained in the famine areas until after the good harvest of 1893, which brought the region back to normal.

In November 1891, the Russian Government ordered that grain would no longer be exported or shipped overseas. By this time, graphic details of the suffering in the famine areas were circulating in the West with reports telling of the famine containing as much detail as possible. Even then, the Russian Government refused to acknowledge the scope of the problem and/or accept aid from outside. In 1892, the Russian government did eventually accept foreign charitable assistance with the result that many lives were saved.

There were also major relief efforts from the United States and other western countries that sent grain and money to the famine area. Western newspapers sent correspondents into the area to report on the situation first hand. They described in extreme detail the horrors they saw, and pleaded for their readers to contribute to the relief effort to help the starving. The Iowa Auxiliary of the Red Cross sent a shipment of corn instead of money because the reporters had described how inefficiently the aid was getting to the peasants. [19]

Sympathetic Philadelphians sent six million pounds of flour that had been collected by merchant millers. The publisher of Northwestern Miller, W.C. Edgar, who assembled a donation collected from states, started this relief. Transportation was provided free of charge by railroads and sent on two steamships from New York to the Baltic port of Libau. Mr. Edgar accompanied the expedition, wrote articles about the situation, and encouraged others to help in the relief.[20]

One of the largest relief campaigns in Russian history was finally undertaken by the government to help alleviate the disaster in which eleven million people received supplemental rations from the state. As Tolstoy had observed and written, the famine proved that the Tsarist government was inept and inefficient in a way that made it incapable of foreseeing the disaster. It also mishandled the relief effort in spite of the tremendous effort that was undertaken. The Russian famine focused attention on the internal weakness and utter backwardness of the Russian Empire. This is not to say that they did nothing. They just did nothing well.

Tsar Alexander III organized a special Relief Committee. He named the Caesarovich, the future Nicholas II, as president. The Emperor himself gave around five million rubles to relief funds while his Empress collected twelve million rubles from foreign donations for the famine areas. The Empress' sister, Grand Duchess Elizabeth, organized her own relief committee that held bazaars in Moscow to sell peasant-made items.

Even with all this, the central treasury with its slow and cumbersome procedures was the main source of famine relief funds. For this reason, aid was extremely slow in getting to those needing it. Compounding this was the lack of adequate transportation or a distribution network. The government distributed special financial aid of 150 million rubles to the people to finance food and seed purchases. They bought food, then loaned it to those who could be expected to repay. However, this "ability to repay" made only some workers and landowners eligible. Sadly, this left the rest of the rural population, consisting of the elderly, children, and widows, excluded.[21]

Flour was distributed monthly to children over the age of two, and to those unable to work. The amount given out would only last between fifteen to twenty days, and due to the lack of fuel, it usually had to be eaten raw. Many were denied aid because the government hoped that they would find work. The government in St. Petersburg did not understand that there was no work to be found.[22]

As usual in these times, the power of the official to choose who received food and who did not (practically deciding who lived and died) was very often abused. Only one-third of the seed that was needed was distributed. Much of what was distributed was eaten instead of being planted. Even if enough seed had been provided, most of the peasants would have been unable to plow since millions of horses either had already died or were sold. This left enormous areas of productive land unplanted.

In February 1892, the government addressed the horse shortage problem by arranging for the purchase of 30,000 horses from the Kirghiz steppes. With all this, the total number of deaths due to the famine of 1891-1892 was approximately

700,000.[23] Even worse, this famine affected the lives of between fourteen to twenty million people.

Was the famine part of a plan to starve out the German-Russians? No, but it was certainly made much worse by man-made circumstances that lead to less food production in farming areas and increased export of what was grown. In 1891, Russia was going through a social shift in rural areas were the number of small farms was reduced while larger farms were increased.

The larger estates tended to grow products for foreign export to earn cash. This was farm collectivization driven by financial factors. The result was that the total amount of food grown in Russia had declined while the amount of exports increased. This change, along with several poor harvests in a short period, made the area susceptible to famine.

Some were opposed to providing aid and saw no problem in the millions starving to death. The future first Premier of the Soviet Union, Vladimir Ilyich Lenin, said:

"Psychologically, this talk of feeding the starving is nothing but an expression of the saccharine-sweet sentimentality so characteristic of our intelligentsia."[24]

This may be when Lenin first realized that Famine would make a perfect weapon. All you had to do was to make famine even worse with bureaucratic bungling, and blame Nature. Sounds almost too simple.

Chapter 4
World War I

With the beginning of the First World War, the situation in Russia for the German-Russians quickly deteriorated. Despite the fact that the Volga German-Russians were loyal to the Russian realm, the Russian Government did not want them living there and did not trust them. The government quickly issued more measures to control them.

German-Russian soldiers serving in the Russian Army were withdrawn from the west front near Germany. The "untrustable" soldiers were instead sent to the fight against Turkey.

Fearing for their safety, an unbelievable number of Volga German-Russians immigrated to other countries. Even so, most of the Volga German-Russians chose to stay where they were.

They were forced to adjust to the ever-tightening control of their daily lives by the Russian dynasty of the Romanov Czar[25]. By 1914, there were still approximately 600,000 Germans living along the Volga River.

It was about this time that the deputy director of the Russian Ministry for Foreign Affairs, Minister Sergei Dmitreyevich Sazonov, called for a "final solution" to the ethnic German problem in Russia.

Minister Sergei Dmitreyevich Sazonov believed that the time had come:

"...to deal with this long over-due problem, for the current

war has created the conditions to make it possible to solve this problem once and for all."[26]

Sergei Dmitreyevich Sazonov [27]

Sazonov was not the only one in the Tsars Government that recommended ridding Russia of the German-Russians. Russian Minister of War General Alexei Polivanov wrote in a pamphlet that stated:

"Russia's Germans must all be driven out, without respect of age, sex, any supposed usefulness, or their many years of residence in the empire."

Russian Minister of War
General Alexei Polivanov [28]

Russian Commander-in-Chief Grand Duke Nikolai was

impressed by the words of Alexei Polivanov in his pamphlet. He strongly supported the anti-German views and ordered the pamphlet distributed among all Russian soldiers.

Russian Commander-in-Chief
Grand Duke Nikolai [29]

In 1915 and 1916, the deportation of ethnic-German groups followed the issuance of property expropriation laws. In all, approximately 190,000 to 200,000 ethnic Germans were deported in 1915-1916. [30]

The Russian government adopted two laws in 1915. They were called "liquidation laws", because both aimed at the foundation of the life of the German settlers, the ownership of land.

The first law stated:

"that all persons of German, Austrian and Hungarian nationality, who had become Russian citizens after 1 January 1880 in a zone of 150 Werst along the border to Germany and Austria Hungary as well as in a zone of 100 Werst had along the coast of Baltic Sea, Black Sea, and Asov Sea, must sell their land their landed property within ten to sixteen months to someone still eligible to own property."

Persons that were of the Orthodox Faith or those that renounced their religion and switched to the Orthodox Faith were able to keep their land and own even more. The Laws were not put into action, but served as an obvious threat aimed at the German-Russian communities.[31]

The First World War completely turned the Russian people against the Volga Germans. The conversion law of January 1917 dissolved the Volga colonies. Deportation was planned for February 1917. A quote from the Bishop of Saratov at that time:

"On February 26, 1917 there was an order sent out by the Czar demanding of the 2,000,000 German people in Russia, all of their grain and goods and cattle and horses that they had in their possession. Upon the fall of the Czarist government, it was found that the Czarist government planned this order with the view to starving and driving all of the German subjects out of the

dominion of Russia. At the time of the fall of the Czarist government, orders were in the hands of the army to proceed with forces into the colonies along the Volga to execute this commandeering ukase.

On that same day, I had urged the boys in my Seminary of Saratov (because there were no men except old men at home) to pray for a miracle to save us from extinction, and on the same day, the revolution began in Petrograd, 1800 mounted Cossacks were held in readiness at Saratov, to swoop down on the defenseless villages, to murder, plunder and scatter the inhabitants. But on account of the revolution the order was never executed."[32]

The Bolshevik Revolution and violent civil war had stopped the order. The provisional government switched to the Orthodox Faith. The provisional government fell, and the Communists came to power. Working with-in Communist Party Soviet rule, the Volga Germans gained some rights and autonomy as non-Russian minorities.[33] However, even though they won some rights, they still lost in the end.

Following the Bolshevik Revolution, the Volga settlements were forced to give up their seed wheat.[34] Approximately 170,000 men, women, and children died of starvation in the German colonies alone.

Chapter 5
Lenin

Vladimir Ilyich Lenin [35]

The Government of Lenin was one of devastation and death. His "subculture of massacre" extended to all areas of Russian control, and the Volga area did not escape.

While Lenin did not personally order each execution or mass murder, he did install and use the Soviet system of terror. Some estimate that between 1915 and 1949, about one million Russian Germans needlessly perished under the last Russian Tsar, Premier Lenin, and Premier Stalin.

Vladimir Ilyich Lenin was born Vladimir Ilyich Ulyanov in Simbirsk, Russia in April of 1870. He was the son of a Russian civil service official who worked for progressive democracy and free universal education in Russia.

Lenin was a Communist revolutionary of Russia, the leader of the Bolshevik party, and the first Premier of the Soviet Union. He was also the main theorist of what has come to be called Leninism, which describes itself as an evolution of Marxism to "the age of imperialism."

Under the leadership of Lenin, the Bolsheviks sought to destroy all religion. The Volga German-Russians were targeted, and severely persecuted because of their religious beliefs.[36]

The first colony to suffer was Balzer. The Red Guards attacked it in December 1917. After this Government supported attack, there was no safe place for the people. Roving gangs of soldiers and criminals used the Red Guards attack as their authority to prey on the people.

The colony of Katharinenstadt was attacked by a hundred Russian soldiers. They extorted large sums of money from the villagers before they left.

City of Katherinenstadt   37

On Sunday, April 17, 1918, the Red Guards attacked the colony of Schaffhausen while most townspeople were in church. The townspeople at first succeeded in driving the Red Guard back, but the Russians eventually retuned with a larger force and seized the town. To make an example, they killed many of the townspeople and drove of most off the livestock.[38]

On July 28, 1918, Lenin issued a decree that established a Commissariat for German Affairs in Saratov. The main responsibility of the Commissariat was to battle the big farmers and the counter-revolutionaries among the Volga

Germans. The Commissariat was also to oversee all requisitions in the area. In reality, he was there to direct the terrorizing of the Volga Germans.

In the late summer of 1918, there was a horrible attack on the village of Dobrinka.[39] Three hundred fifty-three Lutherans from Germany had founded the village, one of the mother colonies, on June 29, 1764. It was located on the 'Bergseite" (hilly side) or west bank of the Volga River, south-southwest of Saratov.[40]

The historical records tell that the village was attacked, and the population robbed. Those that refused to give up their possessions were shot down. Women and children "were raped by the cruel beasts" with several children having died as a result. The records do not specifically say who was responsible for this attack, but they do lead to speculation that the attack was incited by, and if not sponsored or sanctioned by, the Commissariat for German Affairs in Saratov.

More importantly, it appears that both the international community and the Volga German-Russians in the area also believed that the Dobrinka attack was Government sponsored. In September 1918, a diplomatic group from Switzerland, Denmark, and other neutral states protested to the Soviet government about the government sponsored repression and extermination of persons whose only crime was that of belonging to the middle classes.

The Soviet Government's response was:
"(W)e are engaged in a civil war......This counterrevolutionary clique which utilizes foreign and Russian capital to force slavery and war on the Russian people, this clique of Russian workers will ruthlessly annihilate.......(A)gainst our enemies a ruthless war!....

(V)iolence in Russia is used only in the holy interests for the liberation of the masses......"[41]

By 1919, all pastors were considered counterrevolutionary propagandists and were sent to slave camps. Life did not get easier as the Germans felt the harsh changes of collective farming, famine, and political purges.[42]

Rebellion in Warenburg

Whether it was because the Volga German-Russians were enraged about the attack on their countrymen in Dobrinka, or that all their pastors were sent to slave camps, or that their young men were being drafted for military duty, or for some other Commissariat for German Affairs action is not really known, but in January 1919, the people of Warenburg finally said "NO."

The following is a translation of this event by Richard Kisling. The article appeared on page 5 in the August 26, 1920 issue of Die Welt Post with the title "Hochwichtige Kriegserfahrungen der Wolga-Deutschen" or "Highly Important War Experiences of the Volga Germans". That publication gave credit for the article to the May 15, 1920 issue of Heimkehr, a publication from Germany. Note that it appears to be written with a Russian slant or perspective:

UPRISING IN WARENBURG

"A few months ago we received the first reports about a revolt in the large German colony of Warenburg on the Bergseite [sic]2 of the Volga River. We are now in a position to inform our readers of the details about the events in Warenburg. Pastor Schoening graciously placed the information at our disposal for publication. It was supplemented by statements from persons who recently came out of Russia.

The bodyguard of the present Russian government, known as the Red Army, originally consisted exclusively of volunteers. With the further expansion of the Revolution on the borders of the empire in Siberia, the Ukraine, Poland, Lithuania and the Baltic (in which the [World War I] allies soon took part), the formation of a huge army became imperative.

The government was forced to draft non-volunteers into the army and to order a general mobilization. First, in the late autumn of 1918, all of the former officers, noncommissioned officers and sergeants were called up.

Many of these sought to escape but finally had to report, because the government threatened to retaliate against their close relatives. The general mobilization was implemented gradually by province and age group.

As early as the autumn of 1918, several age groups were mobilized on the Bergseite of the Province of Saratov, which had precipitated uprisings in several German colonies.

The German colonies in Samara Province [Wiesenseite] were especially known to the government as a counterrevolutionary element; as a result they delayed the execution of the mobilization decree until January 1919. All men between the ages of 18 and 45 were to be drafted.

This news reached Warenburg on January 3. The local soviet made the mandate of the Saratov German Bolshevik Commissariat known to the community at a town meeting. Those who attended were seized with deep indignation. Warenburg's soldiers gathered together and, after considering and discussing the situation, unanimously resolved not to follow the command of the commissariat.

They made a solemn vow to each other to stand together to the end. An action committee of three people was elected. The leaders of the village council reported this occurrence to the district soviet in Seelmann (Rovnoye) and requested a dispatch of a unit of the Red Guard to carry out the mobilization.

Seventeen Red Guards were sent from Seelmann, two of whom had originally come from Warenburg. The insurgents found out in time and met the Red Guards with a squad of twelve men, with Peter Kaiser at their head. The two groups met outside the village. The Red Guards threatened to shoot. The colonists were equipped only with various farm implements; by that time all weapons had long been confiscated.

They seized upon a trick and announced to the Reds that they were armed with bombs and would use them immediately. The Reds, thus intimidated, were taken prisoner. They delivered up a machine gun with five chests of ammunition, sixteen rifles and over two thousand rounds of ammunition. Then they were locked up in Warenburg.

Five of them, who had voluntarily entered the Red Guard, were killed by the enraged farmers on the way back to the village. In the meantime, the leadership of the local village soviet had telegraphed to Balzer (a nearby village) and asked for help. The commissariat there sent thirty-eight men, all volunteers and on horseback, under the leadership of the teacher, Schaufler.

On January 5 at 10 a.m., this unit approached the village. It had come by way of Achmat and Lauve. As a precaution, Schaufler stayed behind in the latter village. The insurgents were forewarned by the sentinels they had established. In the square in front of the church, they set up the machine gun they had captured the previous day.

As the Reds approached, a shot rang out from their midst. This was the signal for the Warenburgers to attack. They aimed the machine gun at the approaching Red Guards and mowed them all down. Only three wounded [Reds] escaped, and they spread the news of the uprising everywhere. Among the seriously wounded there was even a capitalist, who had joined the Bolshevik army in order to thus save his wealth, but he died of his wounds.

The incidents in Warenburg were telegraphed via Achmat and Balzer to Saratov. The captured material this time amounted to: one machine gun with five cases of munitions; thirty to forty rifles with rounds of ammunition; hand grenades, revolvers and swords.

A regiment stationed in Saratov and made up of Latvians, Russians and Hungarians was sent to Warenburg on a retaliatory mission.

The Warenburgers had already received news about this and had quickly organized battle preparations. There were, in addition, two hundred men from the neighboring village of Preuss, who had arrived ready to help, armed with rifles and agricultural equipment. Both machine guns were set up in Warenburg, and the side streets were blockaded with harrows and other implements.

At 9 o'clock the militia from Saratov arrived. Upon their arrival in the village, fire opened up from both sides. There were many dead and wounded on the side of the Reds. They had to pull back and continued the bombardment in front of the village. The gunfire lasted all day and into the night. Because it was frightfully cold, that is to say 26 degrees Reaumur [sic]3, they pulled back by degrees to the nearest villages. Following this, the night remained calm for the most part.

The next morning at 7 o'clock, the news spread that a regiment of support troops from Pokrovsk [Engels] was advancing with three field guns (cannons). Simultaneous with the arrival of the Pokrovsk troops, eighty-six men from the German Commissariat in Saratov also appeared. The Warenburgers saw that they were no match for this superior power; their will to resist weakened. The auxiliaries from neighboring Preuss marched off in view of this event. The position of the Warenburgers became untenable.

The Reds sent in an emissary right away that same morning at about 10 o'clock to ask whether or not the Warenburgers would surrender. The farmers wanted peace, which was assured them with the surrender of all of their weapons. At that point, the aforementioned regiment advanced into the village, which was already surrounded by troops.

After the [Red] prisoners, about ninety men, were freed by the Latvian regiment, the commander said, "Now we'll show them!" That was the signal for general plundering. All who had taken part in the uprising were taken prisoner. Seven men were shot immediately. About ninety men were killed in all. On Wednesday, January 8, Schutz, the investigating magistrate, came from Saratov, and the terrible trial began.

All who were under suspicion of participating in the uprising in any way were brought forth. About thirty men were placed on the mountain slope of the village and likewise shot. All their possessions were confiscated. The wives and children of those involved had to leave their homes just as they were. Homeless in the middle of winter, they sought shelter with friends and relatives.

Damages of 1,300,000 rubles were levied against the colony. The sum that each had to pay individually was specified. Anyone who refused or could not raise the money was to be shot. The retribution was paid in two hours. About four to five million rubles were confiscated. The worst treatment was to those who had Schutzscheine [certificates of protection] from the German Empire. Five who had been sentenced to death escaped.

A bounty of 10,000 [rubles] was placed on their heads. The systematic plundering of the village continued all that day and the following day. Many sheep, 380 horses, nearly 200 cows, camels and other livestock, poultry, food supplies and clothing were expropriated.

One of the fugitives, Wormsbecher, who had been at the head of the insurrection, was discovered and brought in on the 10th. He was terribly mistreated on the way back to the village, with a rope around his neck tied to a sled, which he had to run along beside. He was to be hanged immediately. Wormsbecher was hanged on the large church square.

We further excerpt from the German [language] newspaper Nachrichten, the communist organ published in Saratov, the official account of the uprising.

Record of the Special
Investigation Commission

Those present were Comrades Saranzev, Ostroglasov, Ebenholz, Schoenfeld, Alfred Schutz, Eduard Schutz, Johann Zitzer and Schulz Grab. Individuals were named with the distribution of duties: as Commander of all Troops Present and President of the Collegium, Comrade Nachalov and Comrade Ebenholz; as Investigative magistrates, the Comrades Eduard Schutz and Hermann Schutz; Director in Charge of Arrests, Comrade Zitzer; Deputy President, Comrade Schoenfeld; Administrator of Finances, Comrade Reichert; Commander of Those Arrested, Comrade Ostroglasov; Secretary, Alfred Schutz.

Because of their active participation in the uprising [the following men] were judged and condemned to death by shooting:

Heinrich Trippel
Friedrich Hammel
Alexander Hart
Georg Kraft
Heinrich Gabel [Goebel]
Philipp Hubert
Georg Werner
Konrad Roth
August Kramer
Heinrich Roth
Heinrich Hartwig
Philipp Pfeifer

Andreas Eisner
Heinrich Michael Hartwig
David Schutz
Alexander Pfeiffer
Johann Schutz
Heinrich Schutz
Johann Pfeiffer
Jacob Rasch
Philipp Adolf
Friedrich Schmal
Heinrich Bier
Eduard Simon
Philipp Becker
Heinrich Schpomer [sic]
[Spomer]
Philipp Schpomer [sic]
[Spomer]
Johann Braun
Friedrich Simon
Heinrich Eisener [Eisner]
Johann Stamm
Jaeger Wagenleiter
[Wagenleitner]
Michael Funkner
Heinrich Stuppel

Others who were convicted (but
escaped):
Friedrich Klein
Philipp Doering
Peter Kaiser (father)
Peter Kaiser (son)
Friedrich Krikau
Peter Schmidt

The death sentences were carried out right after the arrests. The property of the condemned was confiscated, as was the property of Vladimir Wormsbecher, whose wife and children were able to keep only the absolute necessities, while the remainder was given over to the Committee for the Poor.

The assessment of 1,300,000 rubles, which was imposed on Warenburg, was apportioned in the following manner: Friedrich Schmall, 50,000 [rubles]; Alexander Bier,50,000; and so on."[43]

This "uprising" was a last act of desperation that ended badly for the colony of Warenburg. The rebellion accomplished nothing, and the number of women and children homeless and left without protection was beyond counting.[44]

Most of my direct ancestors left Warenburg between 1880-1913, not that many years before the uprising. A large number of the men involved were probably my distant cousins, and those listed below were most likely related to me:

Philipp Adolf
Philipp Becker
Peter Kaiser (father)
Peter Kaiser (son)
August Kramer
Heinrich Roth
Konrad Roth
Peter Schmidt
David Schutz
Johann Schutz
Heinrich Schutz

Eduard Simon
Friedrich Simon
Heinrich Trippel
Georg Werner

Chapter 6
Another Famine Arrives

The effects of the Russian Civil War, WWI, and the constantly changing agricultural policies of the new Communist government drastically reduced the agricultural harvests during the years 1915 to 1931. In the fall of 1920 and 1921, widespread crop failures occurred along the Volga River. This was just the beginning of another great famine that would eventually plague the whole area.[45]

During this time, about one third of the population[46] or 166,000 Volga German-Russians starved to death because of this famine. It was caused by three main factors; weather, collective farming, and political purges[47]. Many felt that the Russian government was responsible for these deaths because the Bolshevists allowed the international community to help these victims of famine only after over 100,000 had lost their lives.

Year 1920 was a drought year, but the German farmers had learned from the years of living in the Volga region of the absolute requirement to store up enough food to last at least two years. It did no good. The governments' requisitioning bands took away the complete stockpile of food. With no reserves left, famine was inevitable.[48]

In the spring of 1921, the Volga German-Russians worked the extremely rich "Black Earth" under clear skies. The light winter snows ended and hot weather arrived. When the farmers went to plow and sow their fields, all they found was dry, cracked mud. They plowed and sowed their seed anyway, and prayed for rain. It did not come. The Russian Famine that began in 1921 and ended in the summer of 1923 was one of the worst disasters in the area's history.[49] Many formerly prosperous and well off Volga Germans found themselves to be paupers, and were forced to become vagabonds and beggars.[50]

The following is from Alexandra Rakhmanova's diary August 15, 1921:

"The train moves slowly, passing endless evacuation trains from the famine areas of the Volga and the North. The cattle trains are crowded with people, piled up like coal: men, women, children. But are this still people? Many of them lost their teeth, their gums are bleeding, their faces are green and ash-gray."[51]

Reports of the terrible conditions made the newspaper headlines. One reporter wrote:

"We went down to the shore of the Volga, down a rough broken street, past booths where you could buy white bread, and, not a hundred yards away, found an old woman cooking horse dung in a broken saucepan. Within sight of the market was a mass of refugees, men, women, and children, with such belongings as they had retained in their flight from starvation, still starving, listlessly waiting for the wagons to move them away to more fortunate districts. Some of them are sheltered from the rain that is coming now, too late, by the roofs of open-sided sheds. Others are sitting hopelessly in the open, not attempting to move, not even begging. I shall never forget the wizened dead face, pale green of a silently weeping little girl, whose feet were simply bones over which was stretched dry skin that looked like blue-black leather. And she was one of hundreds.

A fortnight ago there were twenty thousand waiting beside the quays of Samara. Every day about 1,400 are taken off in wagons. There are, of course, no latrines. The beach was black with excreta until, as an eye-witness (not a Communist) told me, the local Communists arranged a 'Saturdaying' which deserves a place in history, and themselves removed that disgusting ordure, and, for a day or two, lessened the appalling stench that is beginning once more to rise from the beach.

In the morning of the second day we called at one of the sixty "children's houses" in Samara, so that Ercole could photograph the famine orphans, the children purposely abandoned in the streets, in the state in which they were received. The garden, a plain courtyard with a few trees, was full of children lying in the sun under the wall, staring in silent unchildlike groups, ragged, half-naked, some with nothing whatever but a shirt. All were scratching themselves. Among these children, a man and a woman were walking about, talking quietly to them, and carrying sick children into the house, bringing others out.

Ercole had hardly begun to turn the handles of his machine before some of the children saw us, and, some with fright, some with interest, all scrambled to their feet, although many of them fell again, and, too weak to get up, stayed sitting on the ground where they fell. Ercole photographed them as they were. Then he picked four little boys and photographed these alone. Wishing to reward them, he gave them some chocolate before the woman looking after them had time to stop him. "You must not do it," she said; "they are too hungry." But it was already too late. All of them who had strength to move were on top of each other, fighting for the scraps of chocolate like little animals, with small, weak, animal cries.

That is only one of dozens of such scenes that we witnessed during those two days in Samara. Samara is one place of hundreds. Everywhere people are trying to save the children. Nowhere have they the means that we in other countries have to give what they should be given. And, to the shame of humanity, there are some in Western Europe who have urged that help should not be given. Outside the goods station is a huge camp of white tents, a military camp of the Red Army, handed over bodily by the army authorities for the use of the refugees. The refugees have over-flowed from the tents and built more tents, and wigwams for themselves out of anything that came handy - rags, branches of trees, pieces of old iron from the railway sidings.

Everywhere on the open ground outside the cemetery, whither every day fresh bodies are carried ('Thirty-five this morning,' a man told us, whose little hut commanded the entrance to the cemetery), and along the railway line for half a mile or so, were little camp fires, and people cooking scraps of pumpkin rind, scraps of horse-dung, here and there scraps of bread and bits of cabbage. In all that vast crowd there was not one who did not look actually hungry, and for many mere hunger would be a relief.

Among them from tent to tent walked an unshaven young man with a white forage cap, now nearly black, a blue shirt and breeches, and no coat. A mechanic who was carrying the camera tripod for us told me who he was. He was a German, one-time prisoner of war, now a Communist, and 'for all that,' as my man put it, 'a man of God. He has stayed since the beginning. He never leaves them. I don't believe he ever sleeps. Whatever can be got for them he gets it. He has taken and lived through all their diseases. It is owing to that one man that there is such order in this place instead of pandemonium. Thousands owe their very lives to him. If only there were a few more like that.' I wished to speak to that young German, but, just as I was making my way to him through the crowd, a little skeleton of a boy pulled at his sleeve and pointed to a tent behind him. The young man turned aside and disappeared into the tent. As I walked by the tents, even without going into them, the smell of dysentery and sickness turned my stomach like an emetic.

CHILD OF FAMINE   52

A little crowd was gathered beside a couple of wooden huts in the middle of the camp. I went up there and found that it was a medical station where a couple of doctors and two heroic women lived in the camp itself fighting cholera and typhus. The crowd I had noticed were waiting their turns for vaccination. At first the people had been afraid of it, but already there was no sort of difficulty in persuading them to take at least this precaution, though seemingly nothing will ever teach them to keep clean. The two women brought out a little table covered with a cloth and the usual instruments, and the crowd already forming into a line pressed forward. I called to Ercole and he set up his camera. One of the sisters called out 'Lucky ones to-day; vaccination and having your pictures taken at the same time,' and while the camera worked, those behind urged those in front to be quick in taking their rags off, and to get on so that they too would be in time to come into the picture.

There were old men and women, girls and little ragged children. Shirt after shirt came off, showing ghastly bags of bones, spotted all over with bites and the loathsome scars of disease. And, dreadful as their condition was, almost all showed an interest in the camera, while I could not help reflecting that before the pictures are produced some at least of them will have left the camp and made their last journey into the cemetery over the way, the earth of which, as far as you could see, was raw with new-made graves.

In the siding beyond the camp was a refugee train, a sort of rolling village, inhabited by people who were for the most part in slightly better condition than the peasants flying at random from the famine. These were part of the returning wave of that flood of miserable folk who fled eastwards before the retreating army in 1915 and 1916, and are now uprooted again and flying westwards again with the whip of hunger behind them.

To understand the full difficulty of Samara's problem it is necessary to remember the existence of these people who are now being sent back to the districts or the new States to which they belong. They have prior right to transport, and, in the present condition of Russian transport, the steady shifting of these people westwards still further lessens the means available for moving the immediate victims of the drought.

I walked from one end of the train to the other. It was made up of cattle trucks, but these trucks were almost like huts on wheels, for in each one was a definite group of refugees and a sort of family life. These folks had with them their belongings, beds, bedding, chests of drawers, rusty sewing machines, rag dolls. I mention just a few of the things I happened to see. In more than one of the wagons I found three or four generations of a single family - an old man and his still more ancient mother struggling back to the village which they had last seen in flames as it was set on fire by the retreating army, anxious simply, as they said, 'to die at home,' and with them a grandson, with his wife (married here) and their children.

ANOTHER CHILD   53

Families that had lost all else retained their samovar, the central symbol of the home, the hearth of these nomads; and I saw people lying on the platform with samovars boiling away beside them that must have come from West of Warsaw and traveled to Siberia and back.

In the doorway of one truck I found a little boy, thinner than any child in England shall ever be, I hope, and in his hand was a wooden cage, and in the cage a white mouse, fat, sleek, contented, better off than any other living thing in all that train. There were a man and his wife on the platform outside. I asked them where they were going. 'To Minsk,' said the man, 'those of us who live; the children are dying every day.' I looked back at the little boy, warming his mouse in the sun. The mouse, at least, would be alive at the journey's end."[54]

Another reporter wrote in early November 1921:

"Saratov, Russia - As one proceeds up the Volga River, the faces of the inhabitants grow thinner, their death lists increase from hunger, malaria and cholera and make the traveler involuntarily recall the "black death" which originated here in the Middle Ages. Thus far there has been no emigration from the city of Saratov but there are 50,000 refugees living in squalor about its river front streets. They have flocked in from the country or are waiting transportation westward. An incident typical of the speculation which takes place amid this struggle for life occurred at Uvek, below Saratov, when the man in charge of two food cars of the American Relief Administration told the correspondent that his cars had not been ferried across the river to the village of Pagashusk because the station master wanted either part of the food for himself or a cash tip.

TO THE FOOD LINES

At this point on the Volga, the first food-begging began. Barefooted children who were huddled together on the lower decks wandered about the steamer knocking on doors and windows and begging bits of bread. An Italian opera singer going to Samara played the piano and sang the finale of Tosca in the grand saloon until a crowd collected and then asked for bread saying he (sic) had none for three days.

At a German colonist town of Baronsk, formerly a grain center where there are dozens of empty transit granaries, it was said that five to ten persons were daily dying of hunger and malaria, and that last year's scanty crop had been requisitioned by the Bolsheviki who had not left enough for seed grain last summer. Bread costs 8,000 rubles a pound there.

At Baronsk also were 16,000 peasant children whose mothers were unable to feed them. The Soviet had requisitioned the best houses to shelter them and was serving soup to them daily.

At the once wealthy town of Volsk where the smokeless chimneys of the Portland Cement Works stand on the bleak chalk bluffs above the river, the traveler was met with customary complaints of no medicines and no money to buy food. People meeting the steamer offered their home treasures for food or money. There was signs of pitiful attempts to make use of the Volga River water during the rainless summer to irrigate miles of cabbage patches between the low water and high water marks.

Area of 1921 Famine [56]

The market and shops of the town were closed. The only vestige of pre war activity was at the cathedral where services were held as usual and the vesper bells called to thin-faced people across the triangular square. "When will the Americans come?" queried an old man with a world of anxiety in his voice as he hobbled toward the church door."[57]

Families Fleeing Famine on the Volga River [58]

Between 1920 and 1921, approximately 72,000 people in the Volga Colonies fled their villages towards the western borders of Russia in an attempt to escape the Famine.[59]

MOVING THE BODIES [60]

47

Chapter 7
Volga Relief Society

Family and friends in the United States received letters from their relatives in Russia describing the terrible conditions. As a result of these letters, relief societies were organized in many different states in which the German-Russians had settled. The Volga Relief Society helped immensely by feeding 60,000 adults and 75,000 children, and by distributing medicine, shoes, and warm clothing. The various relief societies reported that German-Russians living in the United States raised approximately one-half million dollars. This was sent to their friends and families still in the Volga area as cash, or as food and clothing drafts.[61]

The Volga Relief Society was organized on August 11, 1921, in the Zion Congregational Church of Portland, Oregon. Former residents of the colony of Norka who had earlier migrated to America originally formed the Society. About the same time that the Oregon group formed, other groups of concerned Germans in Fresno, California and Lincoln, Nebraska were also meeting to learn what they could do to help.[62] Families in America, especially in Portland, Oregon; Fresno and surrounding towns in California; and Lincoln, Nebraska, donated large sums of money to help save their fellow countrymen in the old homeland.

A series of letters under the heading "The Latest Letters from the Volga Colonies" appeared in the "Die Welt Post." Examples give a better picture of the times and tell something of this latter period. Excerpts follow:

"Norka, 15 March 1922. . . On the dark wretched background of the world political situation, the actions of the American Relief Association rise as a shining star. And that applies also to the Volga Relief Society in less measure. It should remain for all time unforgettable here in the Volga Colonies, what you former sons and daughters in America have done for the old homeland during this terrible time. . . .

Adults starve daily, children no more in the villages where the American food kitchens to some extent could function normally. There is much criticism of the kitchens. But when one asks the critic, "What if the kitchens would not exist?" Then one receives the answer, "We would have several hundred more children's graves here in Norka." And how many children who no longer laugh and no longer cry. It is a heavy sorrow when people can no longer laugh, but it is still more dreadful when want brings people so far that they can no longer cry. Such dulled inhuman pitiable ones are seen here almost every day. . .

Direct help which friends can give friend are the "Food Drafts." . . . Sadly, also here our transportation is to blame that things don't arrive quickly enough. But what luck and joy these $10 food packages provide, which in Russian pounds contain some 53 lbs. flour, 262 lbs. rice, 10 lbs. fat or 9 lbs. bacon, about 11 lbs. sugar, 3 1/2 lbs. tea and 20 cans of milk. After weeks or months that some have received letters that Food Drafts have been paid, finally comes the distribution notice. All the lucky receivers of such notices gather together and drive to Saratov, where they receive their packages at the A.R.A. warehouse. . . .

What did one not use as substitute tea: There were apple leaves, cherry leaves, dried and roasted pumpkin peels or carrots. Now there is again good tasting tea with sugar in it. One must know the years of deprivation of our country, in order to understand the joy of the precious contents of this package. . . . If one were to give someone here 10 dollars (10 million Rubel) he could buy only half of what he could receive in such a packet. . . . Reverend F. Wacker, Norka Pastor."[63]

By August 1922, the American Relief Association in the Saratov Volga area was feeding approximately one million adults and children each day.[64]

Historians have described the 1921-1923 Famine relief work along the Volga River as the most outstanding act of charity ever performed by the German-Russians now living in the United States.[65]

"America to the starving people of Russia" [66]

"Gift of the American people" [67]

It is estimated that anywhere from 2 to 10 million Russians perished from starvation and disease during this period – many more than the 400,000 deaths of the last major famine of 1891-1892. The droughts of 1921 and 1922 extended over a larger area of Russia than any previous famines, yet that alone does not explain this famine's death toll.

The mass starvation from 1921 to 1924 was mainly the result of the government policy of forced grain requisition. When the Volga German-Russians resisted, they were completely stripped of all grain and mass executions were carried out. Over thirty percent of the Volga German population was deliberately starved before any relief was permitted.[68]

During this mass starvation, approximately 10,000 Volga German-Russian children were taken by force from their parents and given to Slavic families in the Ukraine. They told the parents that conditions were better in the Ukraine, but government was fully aware that famine conditions were even worse in some areas in Ukraine than in the Volga region.[69]

Under the heading, "The Destruction of a Class," Pastor Heinrich Roemmich wrote in 1958:

"The famine of 1921 vividly showed the Communist leaders what the destruction of the propertied class and the violent carrying out of Socialism leads to. Stressing that the govern- ment's requisition policy was the main, if not sometimes the sole cause of starvation--especially in the Volga-German area." [70]

Professor Emeritus of Political Science R. J. Rummel wrote that in accordance with standard legal theory and definition, the deaths of the 1920's famine should be called **"murder."** [71]

Professor W. R. Durow-Wasenmuller wrote:

"The famine of 1921 was well planned and successfully carried out. The drought merely intensified the famine."

Volga-German author Adolf Bersch stated that the 1921 famine was **"artificially prepared"** by the Communist regime.[72]

By 1921, the Civil War in Russia had been settled, and Vladimir Lenin had come out on top. While Lenin was in control, there was another just waiting for his chance. His name was Joseph Stalin. Stalin was a native of Georgia born in 1878. His birth name was Ioseb Jughashvili, but he later changed it to Joseph Vissarionovich Stalin.[73]

Lenin had solidified his power as Communist Party Leader, but Stalin was waiting in the shadows as General Secretary of the Communist Party. Lenin and Stalin had major political differences, and Lenin wanted Stalin out.[74] Lenin supported a limited free market while Stalin believed in total control with an iron-fisted bureaucracy.

Lenin supported the creation of the Volga German Autonomous Soviet Socialist Republic in January 1924. This new Republic was made up of 66% Germans, 20% Russians, and 12% Ukrainians.[75] In contrast, Stalin believed that all power belonged in Moscow and was his to control.

Lenin made plans to eliminate Stalin's growing power, and was to announce them during the March 23, 1924 12th Party Congress. He planned to censure Stalin and remove him as General Secretary of the Party.

Fate had its own plan, and on January 21, 1924, Lenin died. Yet, there was one more chance to remove Stalin. Lenin had left a "Last Testament" with the important demand that Stalin should be removed as General Secretary of the Party.

Stalin - Lenin in March 1919 during more friendly times [76]

This would have ended Stalin's power. But the Politburo made the choice to ignore and cover-up the Last Testament of Lenin, and the General Party never knew of it. [77]

Fate had stepped in again, and a "new sheriff was in town." One can only wonder how different the world would have been if Lenin had lived and Stalin had been removed.

Would more years of Lenin been any better than the years of Stalin? What different events would have happened? How many millions, if any, would have survived?

Chapter 8
Stalin Assumes Power

Joseph Stalin in 1936 [78]

Lenin did die, and Joseph Stalin did come to power. His first move was to eliminate all his former associates so that he had no rivals. The most notable historical accomplishment of Stalin was that he was responsible for the deaths of at least 25 million Russians and minorities (including Volga German-Russians) in Russia. [79]

In 1928, Stalin launched his first five-year plan to boost industrialization in the Soviet Union. The plan was to double steel output and triple both pig iron and tractor production within five years. The money for industrialization was to come from agricultural, with the use of collective farms. His aim was to create modern 'socialist agro-towns' that would produce greatly increased yields.

Stalin's collectivization plan began in 1929 and was violent and brutal. Overnight with no warning, small peasant holdings were merged into giant farm collectives of as large as 247,000 acres. Wages were abolished. Workers were paid thru a system of work points that were a share of the collective's output. As expected, the peasants formed armed rebellions and violently resisted Stalin's plan. They even destroyed their own crops and livestock so that it would not fall into the Government's hands. Stalin's response was extremely severe.

All collective land, agricultural produce and implements were declared to now be state property. Anyone guilty of destroying or damaging them was to be shown no mercy. Peasants were forbidden to leave the countryside without Government permission. Rich peasants (kulaks) were either killed or sent to labor camps. Farming yields fell by 40 per cent. Even so, the forcible seizure of grain was re-introduced and the Soviet Union doubled grain exports. [80]

Chapter 9
Famine Again

Peasants still living in the villages were directed to provide the Government huge amounts of grain that they were unable to produce.[81] The food shortages were worst in the Soviet Union's richest grain-growing areas, including the Ukraine and Middle Volga. Stalin, assisted by his close associate Lazar Kaganovich.[82] Together, they constructed a campaign to crush Ukrainian nationalism and the rebellious Cossacks, who truthfully reported the existence of famine.

Lazar Moiseyevich Kaganovich was the son of Russian Jewish parents, but was a staunch atheist and supporter of Stalin.[83]

Lazar Kaganovich [84]

Since their plan worked so well with the Ukraine, they must have decided that the problem of the Volga German-Russians would be handled the same way at the same time.

In 1931, Stalin allowed relief grain to be delivered to all regions except the Ukraine[85] and the Volga German-Russians. There was enough grain, but it was kept away. As recent Soviet accounts put it, "this famine was organized by Stalin quite consciously, and according to the plan."[86]

Dr. Ronald Hingley (Oxford) was very blunt in his assessment of who was to blame for the victims of the famine. He wrote:

"It claimed some five million further peasant victims – deliberately sacrificed by Stalin, who continued to dump Soviet grain on world markets while those who had grown it were starving en masse. The new dictator was very largely successful in concealing this disaster from world opinion."[87]

Volga German Professor Adolf Gersch wrote:

"The.....famine, which had been knowingly prepared by the Soviet leadership and the Communist Party, and which had as a consequence mortality on a massive scale among the Volga-German population, was also a planned mass murder."

Even Russian Premier Khrushchev admitted the famine of 1933 was an act of "murder" on the part of his government. [88]

Stalin had realized early on the potential benefits of a famine. He decided he could use a famine to crush Ukrainian and German-Russian Volga nationalism. Both groups had become more powerful and assertive about their cultural and political independence. Stalin was not going to allow this to continue as this opposed his style of communism, and his power.

The center of power of both groups was the peasant.[89] Stalin reasoned that if he destroyed the peasants, then collectivization would easily follow. So in 1932, Stalin put in motion a new tactic where he directed an impossible grain delivery target of 7.7 million tons. Later, he reduced it to 6.6 million tons. It made no difference. One survivor was quoted:

"Our village was given a quota that it couldn't have fulfilled in ten years!"

The quotas were a sentence of "death by starvation" for all the peasant families. His war strategy was simple: to force the unwilling peasants into communes, while also destroying the spiritual resources and cultural achievements that supported their nationalism.[90] If they would not go to communes, they could go to the gulags or just die.

Stalin and the Communist Party showed the starving peasants no mercy. The Party used detachments of workers and activists to seize every last bit of produce or grain. This included the seed grain needed for planting. They searched through peasant homes with rods, breaking into walls and ceilings for hidden stores of food or grain. They dug up yards to search for hidden food. They used special animals to sniff out any remaining food. The Party officials knew that if all the food were gone, the peasants would be dead. But they were still alive, so there must be hidden food. [91]

The peasants survived by eating roots. They boiled bark and their boot soles for soup broth. Some peasants started eating their dogs and cats. In response, the Party ordered village officials to bag a "certain quota of dog and cat skins" and went through the village shooting these animals to eliminate this source of food. The peasants began to eat birds and their eggs, so the communist activists organized bird hunts to eliminate that source. [92]

The terrible spring of 1932 was followed by the much worse spring of 1933. Vasily Grossman, a Soviet writer recorded:

"When the snow melted true starvation began. People had swollen faces and legs and stomachs. They could not contain their urine...And now they ate anything at all. They caught mice, rats, sparrows, ants, earthworms. They ground up bones into flour, and did the same thing with leather and shoe soles; they cut up old skins and furs to make noodles of a kind and they cooked glue. And when the grass came up, they began to dig up the roots and ate the leaves and the buds, they used everything there was; dandelions, and burdocks and bluebells and willowroot, and sedums and nettles..." [93]

With no food left, some of the peasants survived on horse manure. It is reported that some even became cannibals and ate their own children, and those of their neighbors that they could kidnap.[94] The Italian Consul in Kharkov (300 miles west of the Volga River) reported that there was:

"a growing commerce in human meat and that people thru out countryside were killing and eating their own children".

The Government quickly distributed posters that read:

'EATING DEAD CHILDREN IS BARBARISM'.

An eyewitness noted:

"...the fertile Ukrainian soil was covered with human corpses...I saw how special brigades gathered the corpses from the streets and houses, and carted them to common graves, or simply threw them in ravines."

People were sure that there was food in the cities and desperately tried to flee the countryside. In Kharkov in 1932, the police recovered 250 corpses every morning from the railway station.

Despite the enormous severity of the famine, the Government forbade doctors to put on death certificates that the cause of death was starvation. Because of this, the number of people who died during the famine cannot be accurately determined. It is estimated that between two and seven million people (Germans and Russians) died in Russia from this Stalin directed famine.[95]

Famine Area of Ukraine & the Volga Colonies [96]

Stalin had achieved his goal and whole villages were now lifeless. Any that survived were too weak to think about independence or challenging the power of the Communist Party. Having decisively won, Stalin benevolently ended the quotas in March 1933. In April 1933, Stalin had some army grain reserves released for distribution to the dying peasants.[97]

The indigenous Russians, Ukrainian peasants, and Volga German-Russians that survived probably felt that life improved somewhat after this famine. The records show that the Volga German colonies suffered a loss of between 15 to 20% of their population because of the famine. Even worse were the Ukrainian peasants with over 25% of their people dead. Stalin knew he had beaten the Ukrainians, and so he left them alone.

Stalin was still not finished with the Volga German-Russians. He was just warming up to his final solution - The Eradication and Genocide of the all German-Russians.

Chapter 10
Russian (Stalin) Paranoia

The rise to power in Germany of Hitler and his Nazi party worried Stalin about the loyalty of the Volga German-Russians. Some feel that this might be the reason for the purges of 1936 through 1938.[98] However, all of Russia suffered from these purges, not just the Volga German-Russians.

By 1938, the Stalinist terror had slaughtered over 3 million people (including all of Stalin's rivals and their families).[99] Russia had become crazy and paranoid, and the German language was forbidden except in the Volga region.

The Volga German Autonomous Soviet Socialist Republic Prime Minister, the Republic President, and other officials of the Volga government were arrested in 1937. They were not alone since by 1939, there were 18,572 German-Russians in "Corrective" Labor Camps.[100]

At the same time the Volga German-Russians were being imprisoned, they were also being praised. The *Moscow News* wrote in 1939:

"These people are demonstrating to the whole world what the industrious, gifted German people are capable of when they are free of the yoke of Capitalism."[101]

In 1939, a large-scale population exchange between Russia and Germany was planned following the Non-Aggression Pact signed between the Soviet Union and Germany. Many Germans from other parts of Russia did move back to areas closer to Germany. Almost none of the Volga German-Russians were able to move before Hitler broke the pact and invaded the Soviet Union on June 22, 1941.

When World War II began, the Volga German Russians were the oldest, largest, and most densely populated group of Germans in the Soviet Union. The Volga German-Russians were trapped in a country that:

1) viewed them to be the same as Hitler and the Nazis.[102]

2) was obsessed with the task that all Germans must be destroyed.

Stalin did not trust the loyalty of the 300,000 Volga German-Russians deep in Russian territory, and quickly made plans for their immediate deportation after the wars' start. He needed some reason to "legitimize" his deportation plan. Within one month, the Soviet Government performed a series of large-scale "loyalty tests" in the Volga region.

In one of the tests, a detachment of Soviet security police disguised themselves as German soldiers and parachuted into the city of Engles. They wanted to learn the peoples' response, and determine whether the German-Russians were truly loyal to Germany or Russia. Dressed as German soldiers and speaking fluent German, they were met with friendly greetings in some villages. In those disloyal villages, they killed the people and confiscated or destroyed their property. Not everyone was fooled,[103] but enough were. Stalin had his excuse for further action (as if he really needed one). He judged all German-Russians of the Volga Colonies "collectively guilty" of spying for the enemy[104] and of disloyalty.

Chapter 11
Deported to Die

Moscow issued the Ukaz no. 21-160 order[105] that banished all Volga German-Russians to Siberia on August 28, 1941. The government publicly announced that it was going to deport the entire Russian-German population living in the Volga region in this order. This was over half a million men, women and children.[106] The order, signed by President Mikhail I. Kalinin, stated:

"According to trustworthy information received by the military authorities, there are among the German population living in the Volga area thousands and tens of thousands of diversionists and spies, who on a signal being given from Germany are to carry out sabotage in the area inhabited by the Germans of the Volga.

None of the Germans living in the Volga area has reported to the Soviet authorities the existence of such a large number of diversionists and spies among the Volga Germans; consequently the German population of the Volga area conceals enemies of the Soviet people and of the Soviet Authority in its midst.

In case of diversionist acts being carried out at a signal from German by German diversionists and spies in the Volga German Republic or in adjacent areas, and bloodshed taking place, the Soviet Government will be obliged, according to the laws in force during the war period, to take punitive measures against the whole of the German population of the Volga.

In order to avoid undesirable events of this nature and to prevent serious bloodshed, the Presidium of the

Supreme Soviet of the USSR have found it necessary to transfer the whole of the German population living in the Volga area into other areas, with the promise, however, that the migrants shall be allotted land and that they should be given assistance by the State in settling in the new areas.

For the purpose of resettlement, areas having much arable land in the Novosibirsk and Omsk Provinces, the Altai territory, Kazakhstan and other neighboring localities have been allotted.

In connection herewith the State Committee of Defense has been instructed to carry out urgently the transfer of all Germans of the Volga and to allot to the Germans of the Volga who are being transferred lands and domains in the new areas."[107]

A secret second order quickly followed. It described the procedures of how to conduct the deportations, and how to separate any remaining family heads from their families.[108]

Five days later on September 3,[109] the Russian NKVD moved in to the Volga German Republic to replace the existing Government by force. Their goal was to erase any trace of the German people. All German place names were replaced with Russian names. The NKVD surrounded the German villages with troops and went house-to-house to register them for deportation.[110] The Russian NKVD completed the operation 17 days later on September 20th.[111]

Sometimes the German-Russians were not even given the horrible choice of deportation. The NKVD began mass shootings in many villages. Though the actual number is unknown, eyewitnesses reported tens of thousands of deaths.[112]

Officially, the order allowed deportees to take up to 2,000 pounds of personal property per family and an unlimited amount of money with them into exile. No cumbersome items were allowed. They were also required to bring one month's supply of food with them in order to feed themselves while on the journey.[113] Actually they were allowed to bring almost nothing.[114] Some families were given as little as five or ten minutes to pack up their belongings and food for the trip.[115]

Shortly after the September deportation, an official of the Russian Government named Volzhanin went to the now former Volga Colonies. His task was to select and classify the pedigree cattle that the German-Russians were forced to leave behind. He told the following:

"... when visiting many of the empty houses belonging to the German colonists he (Volzhanin) found stale bread and plates of soup covered with mold still set out on the tables, and in other homes saw articles of clothing which had been thrown on the floor, indicating the haste with which deportation had been carried out. The peasant farmsteads still contained cattle which had not been fed or milked for two weeks. A sow and her litter, dying of hunger, lay in one of the pigstys."[116]

And this was after the Russian NKVD and nearby Russian villagers had confiscated almost everything of any value.

The deportees were herded to the nearest rail station and packed 40 to 60 persons into rail cattle cars.[117] The operation included 151 train convoys departing from 19 different rail stations.[118] The operation was handled just as one would handle beef cattle on the one-way trip to the slaughterhouse. In some cases, husbands, fathers and male children were separated and taken away never to be seen again.[119]

Deportation rules for each train specified a commander, a NKVD operative worker, twenty-one guards, a doctor, and two nurses, seven to nine cars for baggage, one medical car, and on train guard car.[120]

Russian mass hysteria had everyone hating the Germans, so there was no one there to protect their "rights" and the rules were not enforced. The Volga German-Russians were kept for two to three weeks in the unheated and filthy rail cars.[121] The insides of these rail cars had only a pail or hole for a toilet. The occupants soon became engulfed in an overwhelming stench of sweat, urine, feces and vomit.[122] Scarce drinking water, overcrowding and unsanitary conditions in the daytime, searing summer heat, and nighttime cold was what all were forced to endure.

During the two to three week trip into exile, many people (especially the children) became ill with gastro-intestinal diseases, mange and measles.[123] These horrible conditions quickly lead to death for many of the old, ailing, and young. Those still living were trapped with the dead in the rail cars until the train stopped. The gut-wrenching stench of decaying corpses of what used to be your loved ones must have driven many crazy.

When the train finally did stop, those that were still strong enough quickly dug graves at the edge of the railroad for their dearly departed relatives' rotting corpses.[124] In some cases, the bodies were left in the overcrowded cattle wagons for weeks.[125] Winter arrived before most reached their banishment areas. With the ground frozen, the corpses of those that died froze solid and were stacked like cordwood on the edge of the tracks.[126] Most estimates indicate that close to 40% of the affected population perished during the trip.[127]

When they finally arrived at their banishment areas, they were considered by the Russians to be sub-humans. The Russians could use them or misuse them anyway they felt.[128] Everyone went into forced labor camps on arrival. Children under the age of 14 were put in orphanages. When they became 14, they too were put to work in the labor camps. Most of the camps were not constructed when the first Volga German-Russians arrived.

The German-Russians did whatever they had to in order to survive, often digging holes as shelter from the weather just as some of their ancestors had done 175 years earlier when they first arrived in the Volga River area.[129] Many that were lucky or strong enough to survive the horrific rail trip, soon perished in the service of the Russians.[130] Since most arrived in winter, the "lucky" survivors usually had inadequate clothing, no shelter, and no means to support themselves in temperatures as low as -40 deg F.[131]

Famine again stalked many of the German-Russian deportees. The Government told them that they could use food vouchers, issued in exchange for their animals taken during the deportation, for a small amount of grain. This was to feed them until they were placed into their assigned collective farms, but it was not until late 1941 that local Siberian authorities began accepting the vouchers.

For the first couple of months in exile, the deported German-Russians only had the food they brought. Some got more by bartering their few belongings with the local Russian population. The starving German-Russians willingly swapped valuable clothes, rugs and utensils for scraps of food. The local Russians felt no empathy for these enemy "Germans." The locals saw a chance to make a profit, and engaged in the regular cheating of German-Russian exiles in trade deals.[132]

The Soviet government was aware that there was not enough food and resources in the deportation areas to keep the deportee population alive, and subsequently many Volga German-Russians only received starvation and death in Siberia.[133]

To the Siberian people, they were only a captive enemy labor source to be used develop the agriculture, mining and forestry of their region. Lack of shelter, food, warm clothing and medical care led to high death rates from not only starvation, but typhus, dysentery, gangrene and tuberculosis. It is estimated that about 20% or 250,000 German-Russians died during the 1940s from these diseases.[134]

The men and older boys that were not killed were separated from their families, moved to the gulag as "soldiers" of a "working army"[135] or "Trud-Army,"[136] and sent away to Siberia. Some of the men and boys from 16 to 55 were hauled off to work on the Trans-Siberian Railroad project. It was so cold there that the men had to keep working in order not to freeze to death. Even so, many lost limbs that froze. Amputations must have been horrible as there was no medical care or painkillers.

Others were put on road construction, in the coalmines[137] of Kuzbas in the Kuznets hard-coal basin[138], the goldmines[139] of northern Kazakhstan and the Urals, or timber felling[140] in the areas of the Kraslag, Viatlag and Usol'lag.[141] Few ever returned from the coalmines.

Women from 16 to 50 cut wood in the Siberian forests or built railroads. If they did not meet their quota of cutting and trimming, they received no rations.[142] Some women and children went for "fishing" to Igarka, to settlements in the

Turukhansk district, to Evenkia, to Taymyr and to settlements along the Angara River.[143]

Freedom to move about was restricted to a limited zone always a few kilometers short of the nearest town.[144] Those that did survive could only live at the poverty level in settlements in Siberia, Kazakhstan, and other areas east of the Urals. They did not have the freedom to leave, and the penalty for leaving was 15-20 years of hard labor in the Gulag camps.[145]

By early 1942, the targeted population had expanded to include the entire German-Russian population of the USSR. By the end of 1942, over 850,000 German-Russians had been taken from their homes and exiled in Kazakhstan and Siberia.[146] By 1952, it is estimated that more than 1.2 million German people had been rounded up and dumped thousands of miles away in eastern and central Siberia or in the Central Asian republics.[147] That number does include the 439,000 Volga German-Russians deported to the Kazakhstan, Krasnoyarsk and Altai Krais, and Novosibiksk and Omsk areas.[148] Some of the Volga German-Russians that had been sent to the "Trud-Army" and still survived were "released" from the camp zones in 1946. The "release" was in name only, as they were still sent into "internal exile" to the same places.[149]

By the end of World War II, the Soviet Government had eradicated or emptied 3,000 settlements, including those in the Volga area, across all of Soviet Russia of German-speaking citizens.[150] After WW II, those Volga German-Russians still living were made to sign contracts with the Soviet government that promised they would never return to the Volga area.[151]

Further illustrating what the Volga German-Russians went through are the following three exile camp reports.

1) From the Colony of Donhof, Exile/Camp Report given by Frieda Andreas (daughter of Iwan Andreas). I selected this report because ANDREAS is one of my ancestor surnames possibly making this one of my relative's families.

"In September 1941 the ANDREAS family, Germans, was deported by the Soviets from the village of DENHOF, canton of BALZER, Autonomous Republic of the Volga Germans: Ivan ANDREAS (son of Jakob) - (1901-1962), his wife Jekaterina ANDREAS (daughter of Ivan) - (1901-1954), their children Andrej ANDREAS (son of Ivan), born in 1926, lives in Kazakhstan), Frieda ANDREAS (daughter of Ivan), born in 1927, lives in Krasnoyarsk, Emma ANDREAS (daughter of Ivan), born in 1928 and Eugenia ANDREAS (daughter of Ivan), born in 1938.

The journey to Siberia by train took about a month. Some of the deported persons were ordered to get off at SON station in Khakassia. The ANDREAS family (and another 8 families, all from DENHOF), were deported to the village of SNAMENKA in the BOGRADSK district / Khakassia. Ivan ANDREAS suffered from asthma and, for that reason, was not called up into the "Trud-Army" in 1942. However, after 9 months of exile in SNAMENKA, in spring 1942, the Communists started to send all German families away to the North. The ANDREAS family got to the village of DVORETS, district of KEZHEMSK, on the river Angara. The exiled remained under military command until 1956." [152]

2) From the Colony of Straub, Exile/Camp Report given by Heinrich Bengel (son of Heinrich). I selected this report because Straub was the home village of many of my ancestors that lived in the Volga region. Had they not immigrated to the United States, this file might be about them.

"In September 1941 the Communists deported from the village of STRAUB, canton of KUKKUS, Autonomous Republic of the Volga Germans, the German farmer's family: BENGEL Heinrich, son of Peter, 1895-1957, BENGEL Kristina, daughter of Alexander, 1899-1970, BENGEL Anna, daughter of Heinrich, born in 1924, BENGEL Frieda, daughter of Heinrich, 1927-1948, BENGEL Heinrich, son of Heinrich, born in 1939.

On 28.10.41, the train with the exiled Germans was unloaded in Abakan, and they were taken on horseback to far-off villages. The BENGEL family came into exile in SAGAYSKOYE, a village in the district of KARATUSK. Among them were about 10 families from STRAUB: the WEISBROTs, the ROOTs, the SCHWABELLANTs, the GLEIMs and the DOOSes. The families of Kristina's brother, Daniel WINTER (son of Alexander), and his sister, Jekaterina BRAUSMAN (daughter of Alexander), were exiled to the village of KARATUS (district town).

Their father, Alexander WINTER, was deported to KLYUKVENNAYA station (today the town of UYAR), arrested there in autumn 1941 on section 58 and died in the NORILLag, as was heard by a roundabout way. Beginning 1942 Heinrich (son of Peter) and the 14-year-old Frieda were called up into the "Trud-Army". They came to KEMEROVO and both worked in the mine until 1946. There Frieda became ill with tuberculosis. Next Anna was sent to the "Trud-Army", however, not to Krasnoyarsk, but to the BUMSTROY (paper works). Kristina was in luck: she was not sent to the "Trud-Army". In fact, mothers with little children were not supposed to be called up; nevertheless, this was done quite often. At the end of their term in the "Trud-Army" Henrich (son of Peter) and Frieda returned to the village of SAGAYSKOYE to live there in exile. Shortly afterwards, Frieda died from tuberculosis.

The elder son, Peter (son of Heinrich) BENGEL (born in 1921), served in the army from 1939. He finished the military college for artillery in Sumsk and became an officer; at the beginning of the war he had to go the front. In autumn 1941 he was taken out of the army, just as all the other Germans; but he was given a service record book, bearing the entry "at disposal for special duty". He went to his family in Krasnoyarsk, without escort, and got to the BUMSTROY by accident (apparently, "Trud-armists" did not live behind barbed-wire fences there). When he mentioned his family name, he was immediately identified by his sister.

Later-on they sent Anna to the lumber industry in SHUMIKHU (today situated out of DIVNOGORSK), and in 1945 she was transferred to MINDERLINSK, to the NKVD "podkhoz" (an agricultural institution/farm that provided the nationalized firms in the towns with agricultural products, such as potatoes, vegetables, grain,...), which today is an "uchkhoz" (a mostly agricultural institution, where the apprentices learn about farming, cattle breeding, but also the repair of machines (plows, harrows,....), situated in the district of SUKHOBUSIMSK. After 1956 she stayed to live there."[153]

3) From the Colony of Donhof, Exile/Camp Report given by Klara Aab (daughter of Wilhelm Aab). I selected this report because AAB is also one of my ancestor surnames possibly making this one of my relative's families.

"Klara's family lived in DENHOF, a village in the canton of BALZER, Autonomous Republic of the Volga Germans. Her father, Wilhelm AAB (son of Friedrich), born in 1906, worked in the cotton weaving-mill in DENHOF (the rehabilitation documents mistakenly mention: solitary farmer). He was arrested by the Communists on 02.11.37, sentenced on 11.11.37 in accordance with the decision of the Troyka of the NKVD of the Autonomous Republic of the Volga Germans and shot dead in BALZER on 13.11.37. He was rehabilitated by the Saratov Regional Court on 31.07.1961. Klara Wilhelmovna familiarized herself with her father's court records No. OF-26326 in May 1990. Actually, the file only shows one single entry "interrogations" - nothing else.

The file also mentions: SCHELER, Peter (son of Jakob), born in 1897, also arrested on 02.11.37 and shot dead on 13.11.37, as well as STOL, Heinrich (son of Heinrich). Wilhelm AAB's brother, Filipp AAB, born in 1899, worked as a joiner just in that factory. He was arrested on 13.02.38, convicted of anti-Soviet agitation on 15.02.38 and shot dead in BALZER on 25.02.38. On the petition of the Saratov Regional Department of Public Prosecution he was rehabilitated as certified on 06.12.89.

On 17.09.41 the Soviets deported the following families from DENHOF: AAB Maria-Ekaterina (daughter of Wilhelm) (1908-1971), widow of Wilhelm AAB, her daughters Emma (born 1928), Klara (born 1930), her sons Viktor (born 1931) and Arthur (born 1937). BECHTOLD Ekaterina (approx. 1880-1943), mother of Wilhelm AAB, and her second husband BECHTOLD Georg (approx. 1875-1942). AAB Elisabetha (born around 1902), widow of Filipp AAB, her daughter Ella (born 1936) and her sons Filipp (born around 1925) and Jakob (born around 1927). BECKER Wilhelm (born around 1906), his wife Maria (born 1901), their children Jewgenia (born around 1927), Frieda (born 1930), Karl (born 1935), Woldemar (born 1938), Erna (born 1941), Wilhelm (born around 1924).

They were en route by train for 17 days, then ordered to get off at SON station in Khakassia, North of Abakan; they were taken to the village of POTEKHINO in the district of BOGRADSK by rack wagons. There the five families lived in the former office building until spring. In January 1942 Wilhelm BECKER and his son Wilhelm were forced into the "Trud-Army". Shortly afterwards the son died. The father returned in 1950 or 1951 and died a few years later. Then they obviously sent Filipp AAB to the KRASLag, in spring 1942 Jakob to IGARKA and the mother - to BASHKIRIA. Ella stayed with the grandmother and when she died, she was taken to an orphanage. Approximately in 1948 Filipp and Jakob returned and it was decided in the commander's office to take them to their mother.

Today she and Ella live in SALAVAT. In 1943 the families were sent to work in the timber industry of the SON region, 9 km away from SON station. This timber factory was transferred to the South in 1950, to the mountainous district of TASHTYPSK, to a village called MALY ARBAT, and the director insisted on having the Germans also transferred there. This demand was not rejected. The members of the AAB family live in Krasnoyarsk, members of the BECKER family in MALY ARBAT and the settlement of Arbasa."[154]

Chapter 12
Did The World Even Care?

During the years from 1941 to 1955, nothing of the deported German-Russians was reported in any publication of the Soviet Union. Their actual whereabouts remained a mystery.

But, what about the rest of the World? Surely, the people of the United States of America, or France, or Britain knew of these atrocities and were outraged.

If not the People, what about the Newspapers? They will report anything that will sell papers.

There was a series of articles in 1931 in the New York Times about Stalin and Russia. Correspondent Walter Duranty wrote the 13 articles. The articles were so well received that Walter Duranty was awarded the 1932 Pulitzer Prize for them.

The articles were full of lies, but because of the prestige of the New York Times, they were believed. Duranty's reporting was based on official Russian Government Propaganda handouts as his primary source of information.

In 1931, he wrote about the forced collectivization of the farms:

"Must all of them and their families be physically abolished? Of course not — they must be 'liquidated' or melted in the hot fire of exile and labor into the proletarian mass."

As for the 1932 -1933 Famine in Russia, New York Times Reporter Duranty described it:

"Conditions are bad, but there is no famine,"

"....you can't make an omelet without breaking eggs."[155]

Correspondent Walter Duranty not only used questionable sources, but also was apparently under the control of Stalin. He wrote:

"Stalin and his associates have carried with them the strongest and most intelligent elements of the Russian people, and have created a national unity and enthusiasm which the Tsarist Empire never knew. They have learnt by their own errors and pulled themselves up by their own bootstraps, and the nation has followed them. ...a heroic chapter in the life of humanity."

New York Times Correspondent Walter Duranty dismissed other correspondents' reports of a Russian famine as:

"bunk"
"exaggeration"
"malignant
propaganda"
"no actual
starvation"

Malcolm Muggeridge, correspondent of the Manchester Guardian gave us some background on the Russian life of Duranty when he wrote:

"Duranty, a little sharp-witted energetic man, was a much more controversial person; I should say there was more

talk about him in Moscow than anyone else, certainly among foreigners. His household, where I visited him once or twice, included a Russian woman named Katya, by whom I believe he had a son. I always enjoyed his company; there was something vigorous, vivacious, preposterous, about his unscrupulousness which made his persistent lying somehow absorbing.

I suppose no one - not even Louis Fischer - followed the Party Line, every shift and change, as assiduously as he did. In Oumansky's (head of the Soviet Press Office) eyes he was perfect, and was constantly held up to the rest of us as an example of what we should be."[156]

In the reporting of New York Times correspondent Walter Duranty, the cause of the Famine (once he admitted that one existed) was "just nature" and nobody really was actually responsible.

Had he told the truth, maybe the World would have acted and saved lives.[157] Maybe he couldn't tell the truth because he no longer could see the truth.

While "John Q. Public" may have been deceived, the United States Government knew the truth. George A. Gordon, Charge d'Affairs, ad interim in Berlin, Germany wrote a memorandum to the U.S. Secretary of State on June 5,1931.

The memorandum addresses an earlier conversation in Berlin on June 4, 1931 which U.S. Embassy employee A.W. Kliefoth had with correspondent Walter Duranty.

On the next three pages are copies of the memorandum from George A. Gordon:[158]

EMBASSY OF THE
UNITED STATES OF AMERICA
Berlin, June 8, 1931.

No. 955

The Honorable

The Secretary of State,

Washington.

Sir:

As of possible interest to the Department, I
have the honor to enclose herewith a memorandum con-
taining the substance of a conversation between
Walter Duranty, the Moscow correspondent of the NEW
YORK TIMES, and a member of the Embassy, concerning
Soviet Russia.

Respectfully yours,

George A. Gordon,
Chargé d'Affaires ad interim.

Enclosure:
1 Memorandum.

Copy to Riga.

861.5017-LIVING CONDITIONS/268

FILED JUL 6 - 1931

MEMORANDUM

June 4, 1931.

Mr. Walter Duranty, the Moscow correspondent of the NEW YORK TIMES, who stopped in Berlin only for one day, left Russia on June 2 for his annual summer vacation. He told me that the situation in Russia was quiet, although the "Right (Communist) opposition" was still patent. Nevertheless, Stalin considered the time propitious to take his annual vacation and planned to leave Moscow within a short time. This year's area under cultivation amounted to about 70 million hectars in comparison with 65 million in the previous year. Unless the country experienced a severe drought the prospects for the new harvest were for a crop somewhat larger and better than last year. In respect to the Five Year Plan, Duranty, for the first time, was exceedingly reticent. He said it was a mistake to have called it a "Five Year Plan," but as the name and idea was Stalin's pet, everybody was obliged to promote it. The shortage of iron and steel and the disorganization of the railway system was a serious matter and if combined with a real drought, as in 1922, it might cause a collapse not of the Soviet régime but of Stalin and the Five Year Plan. Duranty denied

that

83

that the authorities were interested in dumping Russian goods on the world's markets "at any price" merely to undermine capitalism; their sole purpose was to sell their goods. Russia, he added, was actually dependent upon the continuation of capitalism and the maintenance of high prices until such a time when it could stand upon its feet. In the field of foreign affairs, Duranty stated that Russia was much pleased with Litvinoff's speech at Geneva but disappointed because the League meeting had not widened the breach between the "Versailles Peace Treaty states of Europe" and Germany and its friends. The French willingness to negotiate a commercial treaty was greeted with much enthusiasm and regarded as an offset against Germany's "degovernmentalizing" of its relations with Russia (see the Embassy's despatch No. 942 of May 26, 1931). He was unable, however, to offer any explanation for Germany's new attitude towards Russia and until the moment he reached Germany was under the impression that the change was initiated by Russia. In conclusion, Duranty pointed out that, "in agreement with the NEW YORK TIMES and the Soviet authorities," his official despatches always reflect the official opinion of the Soviet régime and not his own.

AWK EM   A.W.Kliefoth.

84

One can only wonder if Duranty was telling the truth when he stated:

"in agreement with the *New York Times* and the Soviet authorities' his official dispatches always reflect the official opinion of the Soviet region and not his own." [159]

If the statement above was the truth, was the New York Times aware of the atrocities occurring in Russia? Were they, at a minimum, morally responsible for some of the deaths caused by Stalin?

Maybe they were aware, and that this was a case of the journalistic integrity of the newspaper being "sold out" so that their correspondent Duranty would continue to enjoy access to Stalin. There is no proof, but certainly makes one wonder…

The memorandum proves that the US Government knew of the problems in Russia, but they did nothing. Of course, it was a strictly Russian internal problem. And we know that the US Government never interferes in another country internal problems…..

It was probably much easier just to look the other way. When Stalin actually moved ahead to the deportation of the Volga German-Russians in September 1941, France had already fallen to the forces of Hitler. Britain was battling for its' life, and the United States was worried about entering the War.

What was the big deal anyway? By December 1941, the United States was in WWII, and their goal was to defeat the Axis that was lead by Hitler and the German people. The German-Russians of the Volga Colonies were just more Germans.

If the Russians killed off a hundred, or a thousand, or 10 thousand, weren't they just doing the Allies a favor? Secondly, the Volga Colony Deportations were really an internal political issue within Russia, and no business of Britain or the United States. Third, the Allies needed Russia in the battle against Hitler's' armies. This was a case of the greater good for their own peoples, and the German-Russians were Russia's problem.

In August, 1942, British Prime Minister Sir Winston Churchill visited Stalin at the Kremlin. At his meeting with Stalin, Churchill asked:

" ... **Have the stresses of the war been as bad to you personally as carrying through the policy of the Collective Farms?"**

Stalin responded:

"Oh, no" he said, "the Collective Farm policy was a terrible struggle ... Ten millions," he said, holding up his hands. "It was fearful. Four years it lasted. It was absolutely necessary ..."

Stalin continued and said:

".. that some peasants agreed to come in with us and were given land to cultivate in Tomsk or Irkutsk. But, the great bulk were very unpopular and were wiped out by their labourers (?)."[160]

Both President Franklin D. Roosevelt and Churchill allied themselves with Stalin. They were aware that his regime had murdered at least 30 million people long before Hitler's had started the extermination of the Jews and gypsies. Politics make strange bedfellows! The photos below show them all together.

161

162

163

164

In some weird way, their reasoning was apparently that <u>only Germans could be guilty of Mass Murder</u>. History tells us that <u>Stalin murdered three times more people than Hitler</u>, and that our President Franklin Roosevelt knew Stalin as "Uncle Joe." The US and Britain alliance with Stalin made his control of Russia that much stronger. To make things even worse, Roosevelt and Churchill handed over half of Europe when the War ended in 1945. [165]

The only leaders that publicly denounced Stalin for the murders and deportations were Hitler and the Italian Dictator Benito Mussolini. What patriotic American or Britain would publicly agree with those two Axis leaders during WW II? So nothing said, nothing done, and the World turned away.

Stalin was free to murder millions, and so he did.

Chapter 13
Reversal of Deportations

In September 1955, fourteen years after the mass Volga German-Russian Genocide occurred; First Secretary of the Communist Party of the Soviet Union Nikita Khrushchev began to eliminate numerous restrictions on the deportee's lives.[166]

Then on February 25, 1956, Khrushchev secretly condemned the deportations in his speech "On the Personality Cult and its Consequences"[167] (commonly known as the Secret Speech). This was a report to the 20th Congress of the Communist Party of the Soviet Union on February 25, 1956 by the Soviet leader in which he denounced the past actions of former leader of the Soviet Union Josef Stalin as a violation of Leninist principles.[168]

Nikita Khrushchev [169]

While this literally shocked the 20th Congress, the Soviet government began the process of "De-Stalinization"[170] and reversed most of Stalin's deportations.[171]

It was only after this "De-Stalinization" did the deported German-Russians living conditions improve beyond the minimal survival level.[172]

Even after the Stalin era treason verdict against the Volga German-Russians was reversed, the German-Russians continued to be controlled by numerous restrictions, such as the ban on return to their Volga homeland.[173] Full implementation was slow and did not occur until 1964.[174]

The Soviet Government publicly issued an official decree (drafted on August 29, 1964) on January 5, 1965. After a little over 24 years, the truth came out in this public announcement when it stated:

"Life has shown that sweeping accusations (namely that thousands and tens of thousands of diversionists and spies were to be found among the Volga Germans) were unfounded and represented an expression of despotic caprice, conditioned by the personal cult of Stalin. The successors of Stalin have now established that the overwhelming majority of the German population have in reality contributed through their work to the victory of the Soviet Union over German, and actively participated in the communist reconstruction during the postwar years."[175]

Under a special arrangement with the German government, Soviet Germans could immigrate to Germany. However, this permission to return to their homelands only occurred after the disintegration of the Soviet Union in 1991.[176] After 1991, the Volga German-Russians (along with other deported groups such as the Crimean Tatars, and the ethnic Georgian Meskhs) were finally allowed to return en masse to their homelands.[177]

By the end of 1995, 1.4 million deported (or descendants of those deported) German-Russians had moved back to their original fatherland of Germany[178] under the Federal Republic of Germany "Law of Return"[179] that recognizes the right of anyone with German ancestry to German citizenship[180]. There were still1.2 million more living in Kazakhstan, Kyrgyzstan and the Russian Federation at the end of 1995.[181]

The Volga German-Russians were free to return back to Germany or the Volga area of their ancestors, or so it seemed. Germany would accept them, but there was a language test to pass. There was also the fact that the individual people in Germany did not really want these "foreigners" back because they really were not real Germans anymore. Real Germans would not have left the motherland in the first place... So Germany was not the "home" that they expected, and being accepted by their native people was not to be easy.

However, there was always the possibility of returning to the Volga area of their ancestors. That was not to be either. When the Volga German-Russians were ripped from their homes and deported in 1941, their productive villages and fields were left empty. This did not last long.

Native Russians moved into the homes and took the property left behind for their own. They adopted the animals and worked the fields that they now owned. They knew that the former owners, those Germans, would never be back. The Soviet government had even renamed the villages so that all traces of the Germans were erased.

When Communist Party Leader Mikhail Gorbachev began his perestroika (reconstruction), the "Volga German problem" became better known. In an effort to make things right, the Soviet government declared their intention of re-establishing the area of the former Volga German-Russians for their present day ancestors. This would be accomplished by making a new Volga German Autonomous Republic or VGAR. This made a lot of sense to the former Volga German-Russians, who rightly viewed the forced deportation of their people as a terrible injustice. This would allow them to return home to their former villages and property to start a good life again.

The problem was that their villages were long gone. The buildings might still be there, but the village had been renamed with Russian names long ago with Russian families living in them for two or three generations. Those Russian families living in the area of the future VGAR believed rumors that they would be kicked out of their homes that they had lived in for generations, but would now revert to their previous owners when the Volga German-Russians returned. Mass movements against the VGAR formed everywhere. They often used openly chauvinistic slogans and tended to equate the Volga German-Russians with the Nazis. Rumors of intentions to stop the "unwanted newcomers" by force circulated. The resistance proved to be too strong and the Soviet government dropped its' plan to build a new VGAR.

Even so, some former Volga German-Russians did resettle in the Volga region. They were not allowed to settle just anywhere, but were forced to live in "shipping container" villages isolated from their former villages. After experiencing all the charms of life in these "container villages" among a hostile ethnic Russian population, many of them changed their minds and left. As word of their new life in the Volga spread, the number of Germans wanting to resettle just dried up. As a result, the percentage of ethnic German-Russians in the population of the Volga River area has remained quite low. Those Volga German-Russians that did stay dreamed of the creation of compact ethnic German settlements in the Volga region, the revival of the German language and culture, etc. They stayed hoping it would come true someday.[182]

On July 15, 1998, Robert Eksuzyan of Reuters News Service filed this story titled "Some Ethnic German Emigrants return to Russia. " About 400 ethnic German families are leaving Germany to return to the Volga region and western Siberia. Most cited their failure to learn German, and rules that restricted benefits to the ethnic Germans in the family as reasons to return. Most of those who returned were farmers."[183]

So where did the former Volga German-Russians that wanted to come back end up. By early 2000, the German government had tightened up the restrictions on those who wanted in to Germany. For example, immigrants from Russia could not choose their city of residence. If they did not cooperate, they were deprived of any financial help. The language tests for immigrants have become incredibly difficult. "In the past one member of the family was required to speak German, while now everyone is required to pass a test, even the old men who had been prohibited to speak German," reported one immigrant.[184] More and more of them have failed in their assimilation efforts and have returned to the only home they know – back where they landed up after deportation in areas like Kazakhstan.

Information from a Balzer descendent, and former Kazakhstan resident, documents many former Balzer family surname lines still live in Kazakhstan. These are surnames of individuals that were resettled there during the forced deportation and their descendants. Among the families who are still represented include Engel, Haberman, Idt, Jakel, Kahm, Kaiser, Klaus, Kling, Lutz, Muller, Popp, Roth, Rutt, and Weber. Others that were from descended from those of other villages include Barthuly, Becker, Decker, Grasmuck, Klein, Meissinger, Ritter, Robertus and Schaffer.[185]

Deported German-Russians <u>enjoying</u> lunch while working the forests of "<u>Scenic</u>" Siberia in 1948 [186]

Summary

Over a 100-year period, the Tsarist and Socialist Governments, and the Russian People enacted laws to deprive not only the Volga German-Russians, but all German-Russians, of their right of self-government, their religious freedom, their right to own property, and finally their right to "live". They used RELIGION to steal their property. They used WAR to kill their sons. They used NATURE and FAMINE to starve them to death. When those did not work fast enough, they became impatient and pillaged, raped, and murdered. The lucky ones were sent to Siberia. The World ignored what Stalin was doing, and was no help. He was free to complete

The Genocide of the German-Russian Volga Colonies.

Forgotten Volga German Grave & Tombstone Warenburg Cemetery 2003 [187]

We cannot forget all they did for us.
Darrel P. Kaiser 2007

Bibliography

1941 Deportation, <http://members.rogers.com/kdee/History/10-Tribulations/Deportation>, accessed 20 July 2005

Aid For Starving Russians, (The Nation, LVI 1892)

Alexei Polivanov, Photographer unknown, <http://www.firstworldwar.com/photos/commanders5.htm>, accessed 30 August 2006

Ali, Tariq, *Trotsky For Beginners*, (Pantheon Books, New York, 1980)

American Relief to Russia, (American Review of Reviews, LIV 1892)

America to the starving people of Russia, Photo from the Hoover Institution Archives

American Volga Relief Society letters and documents, <http://www.nebraskahistory.org/lib-arch/research/treasures/volga_relief.htm>, accessed 11 April 2006

Another Child, <http://www.artukraine.com/famineart/famine10.htm>; accessed 10 April 2006

Artificial Famine/Genocide in Ukraine, <http://www.infoukes.com/history/famine/>, accessed 30 August 2006

Child of Famine, <http://www.artukraine.com/famineart/famine10.htm>, accessed 10 April 2006

Churchill – Roosevelt – Stalin, Photographer unknown, <http://www.dw-world.de/dw/article/0,2144,1478863,00.html>, accessed 30 August 2006

Conquest, Robert, *The Nation Killers: The Soviet Deportation of Nationalities,* (New York, NY: Macmillan Company, 1970)

Deportation, <http://www.stanford.edu/~skij/amintro.html>, accessed 21 September 2005

Dobrinka, <http://dobrinka.wathenadesigns.com/>, accessed 9 April 2006

Edgar, W, *Russia's Conflict With Hunger*, (American Review of Reviews, V, 1892)

Families Fleeing,
<http://www.volgagermans.net/volgagermans/images/Volga%20famine.jp g>, accessed 10 April 2006

Fisher, H.H., *The Famine in Soviet Russia 1919-1923*, (The McMillan Co, NY, 1927)

Franklin Delano Roosevelt Memorial,
<http://www.nps.gov/fdrm/fdr/biography.htm>, accessed 30 August 2006

Geisinger, Adam, *From Catherine to Krushchev: The Story of Russia's Germans* (Winnipeg, Canada; Marian Press, 1974)

Genocide, <http://en.wikipedia.org/wiki/Genocide>, accessed 30 August 2006

Genocide in the USSR, (Institute for the Study of the USSR, Munich, Germany, 1958)

Geschichte der Russlanddeutschen ,
<http://www.russlanddeutschegeschichte.de>, accessed 10 April 2006

Gift of the American people, Photo from the Hoover Institution Archives

Golder, Frank & Hutchinson, Lincoln, *On the Trail of the Russian Famine*, (Stanford Univ Press, 1927)

Grand Duke Nikolai, Photographer unknown,
<http://www.spartacus.schoolnet.co.uk/FWWnikolai.htm>, accessed 30 August 2006

Harms, Wilmer A., *Insights Into Russia,* (Journal of the AHSGR, Lincoln, NE, Volume 26, No. 2 Spring 2003)

Haynes, Emma S., *A History of the Volga Relief Society*, (AHSGR, Lincoln, NE, 1982)

Haynes, Emma Schwabenland, *Russian German History After 1917*, (80th Anniversary of the Free Evangelical Lutheran Cross Church 1892 – 1972, Fresno, Ca, 1972)

Heimatbuch der Deutschen aus Russland, 2000 (Landsmannschaft der Deutschen aus Rußland, Stuttgart, Germany, 2000)

Hingley, Ronald, *A Condse History of Russia,*(New York, Viking Press, 1972)

History of the Russian-Germans, <http://www.russlanddeutschegeschichte.de>, accessed 8 April 2006

History of the Soviet Union 1953-1985, <http://en.wikipedia.org/wiki/History_of_the_Soviet_Union_%281953-1985%29>, accessed 8 April 2006

Hoffman, Stefanie, *From Puppets of Stalin to Pawns of Hitler & Back Again: Experiences of Soviet Citizens of German Ethnicity During & After the Second World War*, (Journal of the AHSGR, Lincoln, NE, Volume 28, No. 1 Spring 2005)

Jan. 17, 1993, recorded by V.S Birger, Krasnoyarsk, "Memorial" society, <http://www.memorial.krsk.ru/eng/Dokument/Svidet/Bengel.htm>, accessed 9 April 2006

Joseph Stalin,<http://en.wikipedia.org/wiki/Joseph_Stalin>, accessed 21 August 2006

Joseph Stalin, Photographer unknown, <http://www.fdrlibrary.marist.edu/>, accessed 30 August 2006

Katharinenstadt, Photographer unknown, (80th Anniversary of the Free Evangelical Lutheran Cross Church 1892 – 1972, Fresno, Ca, 1972)

Kazakhstan: Special Report on Ethnic Germans,
<http://www.irinnews.org/S_report.asp?ReportID=45321&SelectRegion=
Central_Asia>, accessed 9 April 2006

Kessler, Bishop Joseph, *Knights Of Columbus Hall Speech,* (Ellis County
News, Kansas- Thursday, February 9, 1922)

Kloberdanz, Timothy J., *The Germans from Russia: A Viable Ethnic
Group or a Fading Phenomenon?,* (Journal of the AHSGR, Lincoln, NE,
Volume 27, No. 1 Spring 2004)

Koch, Fred, *The Volga Germans: in Russia and the Americas, from 1763
to the Present,* (University Park, PA: Pennsylvania State University Press,
1977)

Lazar Kaganovich, <http://en.wikipedia.org/wiki/Lazar_Kaganovich>,
accessed 21 August 2006

Lazar Moiseyevich Kaganovich, Photographer unknown,
<http://encyclopedia.thefreedictionary.com/_/viewer.aspx?path=3/3f/&na
me=Lazar_Kaganovich.jpg>, accessed 30 August 2006

Leo Tolstoy, Photographer unknown,
<http://www.answers.com/topic/leotolstoy-jpg>, accessed 30 August 2006

Mace, DR. James, *A tale of two journalists: Walter Duranty and Gareth
Jones,* THE 70th ANNIVERSARY OF THE FAMINE-GENOCIDE IN
UKRAINE, <http://www.ukrweekly.com/Archive/2003/460315.shtml>,
accessed 30 August 2006

Margolis, Eric, *Seven million died in the 'forgotten' holocaust,*(Toronto
Sun, Nov 16, 2003)

May 28, 1990, recorded by V.S. Birger, "Memorial" Society,
Krasnoyarsk ,
<http://www.memorial.krsk.ru/eng/Dokument/Svidet/Aab.htm>, accessed
9 April 2006

Migration News,
<http://migration.ucdavis.edu/mn/more.php?id=1602_0_4_0>, accessed 11
April 2006

Moving the Bodies,
<http://www.artukraine.com/famineart/famine10.htm>, accessed 10 April
2006

*New York Times Statement About 1932 Pulitzer Prize Awarded to Walter
Duranty,* <http://www.nytco.com/company-awards-pulitzer-note.html>,
accessed 30 August 2006

Nikita Krushchev, Photographer unknown,
<http://www.dictatorofthemonth.com/Kruschev/pictures_of_kruschev.htm
>, accessed 30 August 2006

Nov. 28, 1991, recorded by V.S. Birger, Krasnoyarsk, "Memorial" Society
<http://www.memorial.krsk.ru/eng/Dokument/Svidet/Andreas.htm>,
accessed 11 April 2006

On the Personality Cult and Its Consequences,
<http://en.wikipedia.org/wiki/On_the_Personality_Cult_and_its_Conseque
nces>, accessed 12 April 2006

Pohl, Otto, *Ethnic Cleansing in the USSR, 1937-1949,* (Westport, CT:
Greenwood Press, 1999)

Pohl, J. Otto, <http://jpohl.blogspot.com/2005/08/in-our-hearts-we-felt-
sentence-of.html>, accessed 4 July 2006

Population Transfer in the Soviet Union,
<http://en.wikipedia.org/wiki/Population_transfer_in_the_Soviet_Union>,
accessed 9 April 2006

Ransome, Arthur, *Famine on the Volga*, (The Guardian, London, October
11, 1921)

Right of Return,
<http://en.wikipedia.org/wiki/Right_of_return#Germany>, accessed 12
April 2006

Roosevelt – Churchill – Stalin, Photographer unknown,
<http://www.zwoje-scrolls.com/zwoje41/text01p.htm>, accessed 30
August 2006

Rummel, R.J., *Definition of Democide*,
<http://www.hawaii.edu/powerkills/DBG.CHAP2.HTM>, accessed 30
August 2006

Rummel, R.J., *Freedom Promotes Wealth and Prosperity,*
<http://www.hawaii.edu/powerkills/WF.CHAP4.HTM>, accessed 30
August 2006

Rummel, R.J., *Lethal Politics*,
<http://www.hawaii.edu/powerkills/USSR.CHAP.1.HTM>, accessed 30
August 2006

Russians in Exile, <http://www.joebattsarm.com/lexicografie/dias9.html>,
accessed 12 April 2006

Russia's Ethnic Germans Who Live in Germany Want Back Home,
<http://english.pravda.ru/society/2002/08/28/35468.html>, accessed 11
April 2006

Saul, Norman, *Concord and Conflict, The United States and Russia, 1867-1914*

Schreiber, Steven, *Volga Relief Society*,
<http://www.volgagermans.net/volgagermans/Volga%20Relief%20Societ
y>, accessed 5 May 2005

Schwabenland, Emma, *A History of the Volga Relief Society* (AHSGR,
Lincoln, NE, 1982)

Sergei Dmitreyevich Sazonov, Photographer unknown,
<http://cnparm.home.texas.net/Wars/JulyCrisis/JulyCrisis03.htm>,

accessed 30 August 2006

Sinner, Samuel D., *The Open Wound - The Genocide of German Ethnic Minorities In Russia and the Soviet Union, 1915-1949---And Beyond*, (Germans From Russia Collection, North Dakota State University Libraries, Fargo, North Dakota, 2000)

Sinner, Samuel, 28 August 2005, Portland, Oregon

Stalin and Lenin, Photographer unknown, <http://www.vestnik.com/issues/2003/1015/win/melamed.htm>, accessed 30 August 2006

Stalin – Roosevelt – Churchill, Photographer unkown, <http://www.churchill-society-london.org.uk/1943SOND.html>, accessed 30 August 2006

Starvation is Worse Fyrther into Provinces – Death List in Communities Greater as One Proceeds up Volga River, (Daily Pioneer, Mandan, North Dakota, November 9, 1921)

Stradling, J. and Reason, W., *In the Land of Tolstoi* (London James Clarke and Company, 1897)

Stuttaford, Andrew, *The Paper of Record – An apology that is long overdue,* <http://www.nationalreview.com/contributors/stuttaford051501.shtml>, accessed 30 August 2006

Sulzberger, Cyrus L., Wireless to The New York Times from Moscow, Monday, September 8, 1941

The deportation from the Autonomous Republic of the Volga-Germans (September 1941), <http://www.memorial.krsk.ru/eng/Exile/062.htm>, accessed 11 April 2006

The German Colonies on the Volga River-Deportation, <http://www.volgagermans.net/volgagermans/Volga%20German%20Dep ortation.htm>, accessed 12 April 2006

The Great Famine – Genocide in Soviet Ukraine, 1932-33,
<http://www.artukraine.com/famineart/famine14.htm>, accessed 11 April
2006

The History of the Volga Germans,
<http://www.lhm.org/LID/lidhist.htm>, accessed 22 August 2006

The Jamestown Foundation Prism, (Volume 4, Issue 10, May 15, 1998),
<http://www.jamestown.org/publications_details.php?volume_id=5&issue
_id=276&article_id=313>, accessed 21 January 2006

The New York Times Smoking Gun, Holodomor - the Famine Genocide in
Ukraine, <http://www.ucca.org/famine/gordondispatch.html>, accessed 30
August 2006

The Volga Germans, A Brief History <http://www.lhm.org/LID/lidhist.htm>,
accessed 10 April 2006

The Volga Germans-Those that stayed behind,
<http://members.aol.com/RAToepfer/webdoc8x.htm>, accessed 10 April
2006

Tolstoy, M. de Courcel, *The Ultimate Reconciliation* (New York Charles
Scribner's Sons, 1988)

TSAR Alexander II, Photographer unknown,
<http://www.redeemer.on.ca/academics/polisci/Russian_history.html>,
accessed 30 Aug 2006

Uprising in Warenburg,
<http://www.volgagermans.net/warenburg/Warenburg_Uprising.htm>,
accessed 10 April 2006

Village of Balzer,
<http://www.femling.com/gen/balzer/balzer.htm#Village%20of%20Balzer
>, accessed 10 April 2006

Vladimir Ilyich Lenin, Photographer unknown,
<http://www.sahistory.org.za>, accessed 30 August 2006

Volga Famine of 1921-22,
 <http://www.volgagermans.net/volgagermans/images/Volga famine.jpg>, accessed 10 April 2006

Volga German Autonomous Soviet Socialist Republic, <http://volga-german-autonomous-soviet-socialist-republic.biography.ms/>, accessed 1 April 2006

Watson, Fiona, *One hundred years of famine - a pause for reflection*, <http://www.ennonline.net/fex/08/ms20.html>, accessed 10 April 2006

Webster's Ninth New Collegiate Dictionary, (Merriam-Webster Inc, Publishers, Springfield, MA, 1984)

White, Sharon, *German Tombstone in Warenburg Cemetery in 2003*

Williams, Hattie Plum, *The Czar's Germans*, (AHSGR, Lincoln, NE, 1975)

End Notes

[1] *Webster's Ninth New Collegiate Dictionary*, p.511
[2] *Genocide*
[3] Rummel, R.J., *Definition of Democide*
[4] *Geschichte der Russlanddeutschen*
[5] *TSAR Alexander II*
[6] Williams, Hattie Plum, *The Czar's Germans*, p.173
[7] Haynes, Emma S., *A History of the Volga Relief Society*, p.24
[8] ibid
[9] Author unknown
[10] Hoffman, Stefanie, *From Puppets of Stalin to Pawns of Hitler & Back Again*, p.10
[11] Williams, Hattie Plum, The Czar's Germans, p.175
[12] Harms, Wilmer A., *Insights Into Russia*, p.16
[13] *History of the Russian-Germans*
[14] Author created
[15] Stradling, J. and Reason, W., *In the Land of Tolstoi*, p.45
[16] *Leo Tolstoy*
[17] Tolstoy, M. de Courcel, *The Ultimate Reconciliation*, p.22
[18] Stradling, J. and Reason, W., *In the Land of Tolstoi*, p.59
[19] *Aid For Starving Russians*, p.130
[20] *American Relief to Russia*, p.267
[21] Edgar, W, *Russia's Conflict With Hunger*, p.693
[22] ibid
[23] Saul, Norman, *Concord and Conflict, The United States and Russia, 1867-1914*, pp.335-355
[24] Rummel, R.J., *Lethal Politics*
[25] Harms, Wilmer A., *Insights Into Russia*, p.16
[26] Sinner, Samuel, 28 August 2005, Portland, Oregon
[27] *Sergei Dmitreyevich Sazonov*
[28] *Alexei Polivanov*
[29] *Grand Duke Nikolai*
[30] Sinner, Samuel, 28 August 2005, Portland, Oregon
[31] *The History of the Volga Germans*
[32] Kessler, Bishop Joseph, *Knights Of Columbus Hall Speech*
[33] Conquest, Robert, *The Nation Killers: The Soviet Deportation of Nationalities*, p.260
[34] Schreiber, Steven, *Volga Relief Society*
[35] *Vladimir Ilyich Lenin*
[36] *The History of the Volga Germans*
[37] *Katharinenstadt*

[38] Haynes, Emma S., *A History of the Volga Relief Society*, p.28
[39] Sinner, Samuel D., *The Open Wound - The Genocide of German Ethnic Minorities In Russia*, pp. 18 -19
[40] *Dobrinka*
[41] Sinner, Samuel D., *The Open Wound - The Genocide of German Ethnic Minorities In Russia*, pp. 18 -19
[42] Geisinger, Adam, *From Catherine to Krushchev: The Story of Russia's Germans*, p.243
[43] *Uprising in Warenburg*
[44] Sinner, Samuel D., *The Open Wound - The Genocide of German Ethnic Minorities In Russia*, pp.18 –19
[45] Schreiber, Steven, *Volga Relief Society*
[46] *The Volga Germans, A Brief History*
[47] Geisinger, Adam, *From Catherine to Krushchev: The Story of Russia's Germans*, p.243
[48] *Volga Famine of 1921-22*
[49] ibid
[50] Schreiber, Steven, *Volga Relief Society*
[51] *Russians in Exile*
[52] *Child of Famine*
[53] *Another Child*
[54] Ransome, Arthur, *Famine on the Volga*
[55] ibid, *To The Food Lines*
[56] Author created
[57] *Starvation is Worse Fyrther into Provinces – Death List in Communities Greater as One Proceeds*
[58] *Families Fleeing*
[59] Golder, Frank & Hutchinson, Lincoln, *On the Trail of the Russian Famine*, p.88
[60] *Moving the Bodies*
[61] Schreiber, Steven, *Volga Relief Society*
[62] Schwabenland, Emma, *A History of the Volga Relief Society*, pp.39-42
[63] ibid
[64] Fisher, H.H., *The Famine in Soviet Russia 1919-1923*, p.556
[65] Schwabenland, Emma, *A History of the Volga Relief Society*, pp.39-42
[66] *America to the starving people of Russia*
[67] *Gift of the American people*
[68] *American Volga Relief Society letters and documents*
[69] Sinner, Samuel D., *The Open Wound - The Genocide of German Ethnic Minorities In Russia*, p.40
[70] ibid, p.102
[71] ibid
[72] ibid

[73] *Joseph Stalin*

[74] Ali, Tariq, *Trotsky for Beginners,* pp.109-111

[75] Conquest, Robert, *The Nation Killers: The Soviet Deportation of Nationalities,* p.260

[76] *Stalin and Lenin,* Photographer unknown

[77] Ali, Tariq, *Trotsky for Beginners,* pp.109-111

[78] *Joseph Stalin,* Photographer unknown

[79] Harms, Wilmer A., *Insights Into Russia,* p.16

[80] Watson, Fiona, *One hundred years of famine - a pause for reflection*

[81] *The Great Famine – Genocide in Soviet Ukraine, 1932-33*

[82] *The Artificial Famine/Genocide in Ukraine*

[83] *Lazar Kaganovich*

[84] *Lazar Moiseyevich Kaganovich*

[85] Watson, Fiona, *One hundred years of famine - a pause for reflection*

[86] *The Great Famine – Genocide in Soviet Ukraine, 1932-33*

[87] Hingley, Ronald, *A Condse History of Russia,*(New York, Viking Press, 1972): pp.172-173

[88] Sinner, Samuel D., *The Open Wound - The Genocide of German Ethnic Minorities In Russia,* p.65

[89] Rummel, R.J., *Freedom Promotes Wealth and Prosperity*

[90] ibid

[91] ibid

[92] ibid

[93] Watson, Fiona, *One hundred years of famine - a pause for reflection*

[94] Rummel, R.J., *Freedom Promotes Wealth and Prosperity*

[95] Watson, Fiona, *One hundred years of famine - a pause for reflection*

[96] Author created

[97] Rummel, R.J., *Freedom Promotes Wealth and Prosperity*

[98] Pohl, Otto, *Ethnic Cleansing in the USSR, 1937-1949,* p.30

[99] Ali, Tariq, *Trotsky for Beginners,* pp.160-161

[100] Pohl, Otto, *Ethnic Cleansing in the USSR, 1937-1949,* p.30

[101] Koch, Fred, *The Volga Germans: in Russia and the Americas, from 1763 to the Present,* p.260

[102] Pohl, Otto, *Ethnic Cleansing in the USSR, 1937-1949,* p.36

[103] ibid

[104] *1941 Deportation*

[105] Pohl, J. Otto

[106] ibid

[107] Conquest, Robert, *The Nation Killers. The Soviet Deportation of Nationalities,* pp.62-63

[108] Sulzberger, Cyrus L.

[109] *1941 Deportation*

[110] Pohl, Otto, *Ethnic Cleansing in the USSR, 1937-1949,* p.36
[111] Pohl, J. Otto
[112] *Deportation*
[113] Pohl, Otto, *Ethnic Cleansing in the USSR, 1937-1949,* p.36
[114] Geisinger, Adam, *From Catherine to Krushchev: The Story of Russia's Germans,* p.315
[115] *1941 Deportation*
[116] Genocide in the USSR, (Institute for the Study of the USSR, Munich, Germany, 1958): pp.50 - 51
[117] Geisinger, Adam, *From Catherine to Krushchev: The Story of Russia's Germans,* p.315
[118] *1941 Deportation*
[119] Geisinger, Adam, *From Catherine to Krushchev: The Story of Russia's Germans,* p.315
[120] Pohl, Otto, *Ethnic Cleansing in the USSR, 1937-1949,* p.36
[121] Kloberdanz, Timothy J., *The Germans from Russia: A Viable Ethnic Group or a Fading Phenomenon?,* p.19
[122] Pohl, J. Otto
[123] ibid
[124] Kloberdanz, Timothy J., *The Germans from Russia: A Viable Ethnic Group or a Fading Phenomenon?,* p.19
[125] *1941 Deportation*
[126] Kloberdanz, Timothy J., *The Germans from Russia: A Viable Ethnic Group or a Fading Phenomenon?,* p.19
[127] *1941 Deportation*
[128] Kloberdanz, Timothy J., *The Germans from Russia: A Viable Ethnic Group or a Fading Phenomenon?,* p.19
[129] *Kazakhstan: Special Report on Ethnic Germans*
[130] Kloberdanz, Timothy J., *The Germans from Russia: A Viable Ethnic Group or a Fading Phenomenon?,* p.19
[131] *1941 Deportation*
[132] Pohl, J. Otto
[133] *Deportation*
[134] Pohl, J. Otto
[135] *Kazakhstan: Special Report on Ethnic Germans*
[136] *The deportation from the Autonomous Republic of the Volga-Germans (September 1941)*
[137] *The Volga Germans-Those that stayed behind*
[138] *The deportation from the Autonomous Republic of the Volga-Germans (September 1941)*
[139] *Deportation*
[140] *The Volga Germans-Those that stayed behind*

[141] *The deportation from the Autonomous Republic of the Volga-Germans (September 1941)*
[142] *The Volga Germans-Those that stayed behind*
[143] *The deportation from the Autonomous Republic of the Volga-Germans (September 1941)*
[144] *1941 Deportation*
[145] ibid
[146] Pohl, J. Otto
[147] *1941 Deportation*
[148] *Population Transfer in the Soviet Union*
[149] *The deportation from the Autonomous Republic of the Volga-Germans (September 1941)*
[150] Kloberdanz, Timothy J., *The Germans from Russia: A Viable Ethnic Group or a Fading Phenomenon?*, p.19
[151] *Volga German Autonomous Soviet Socialist Republic*
[152] *Nov. 28, 1991*
[153] *Jan. 17, 1993*
[154] *May 28, 1990*
[155] *New York Times Statement About 1932 Pulitzer Prize Awarded to Walter Duranty*
[156] Mace, DR. James, *A tale of two journalists: Walter Duranty and Gareth Jones*
[157] Stuttaford, Andrew, *The Paper of Record – An apology that is long overdue*
[158] *The New York Times Smoking Gun*
[159] ibid
[160] *Artificial Famine/Genocide in Ukraine*
[161] *Stalin – Roosevelt – Churchill*
[162] *Franklin Delano Roosevelt Memorial*
[163] *Roosevelt – Churchill – Stalin*
[164] *Churchill – Roosevelt – Stalin*
[165] Margolis, Eric, *Seven million died in the 'forgotten' holocaust*
[166] *The German Colonies on the Volga River-Deportation*
[167] *Population Transfer in the Soviet Union*
[168] *On the Personality Cult and Its Consequences*
[169] *Nikita Krushchev*
[170] *History of the Soviet Union 1953-1985*
[171] *Population Transfer in the Soviet Union*
[172] Pohl, J. Otto
[173] *Kazakhstan: Special Report on Ethnic Germans*
[174] *The German Colonies on the Volga River-Deportation*
[175] Haynes, Emma Schwabenland, *Russian German History After 1917*, pp.142 – 145
[176] *The German Colonies on the Volga River-Deportation*

[177] *Population Transfer in the Soviet Union*
[178] *The German Colonies on the Volga River-Deportation*
[179] *Right of Return*
[180] *Volga German Autonomous Soviet Socialist Republic*
[181] *The German Colonies on the Volga River-Deportation*
[182] *The Jamestown Foundation Prism*
[183] *Migration News*
[184] *Russia's Ethnic Germans Who Live in Germany Want Back Home*
[185] *Village of Balzer*
[186] *Heimatbuch der Deutschen aus Russland, 2000*
[187] White, Sharon, *German Tombstone in Warenburg Cemetery in 2003*

Books by Darrel P. Kaiser
www.DarrelKaiserBooks.com

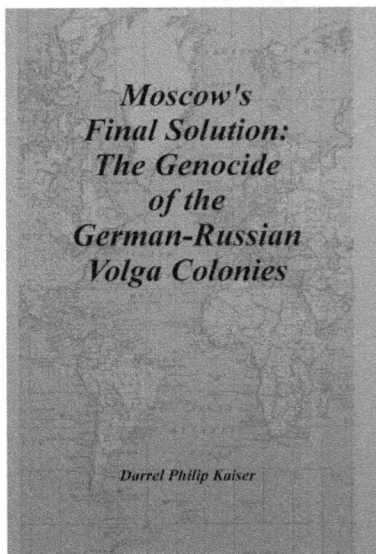

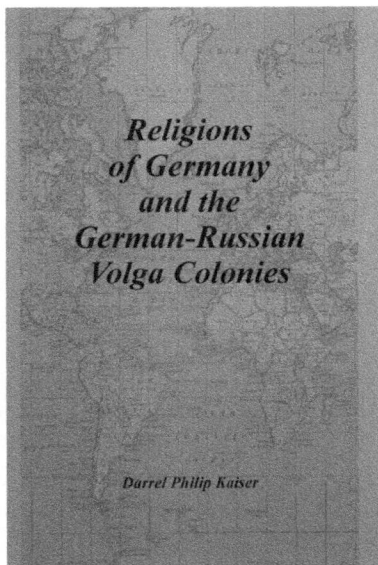

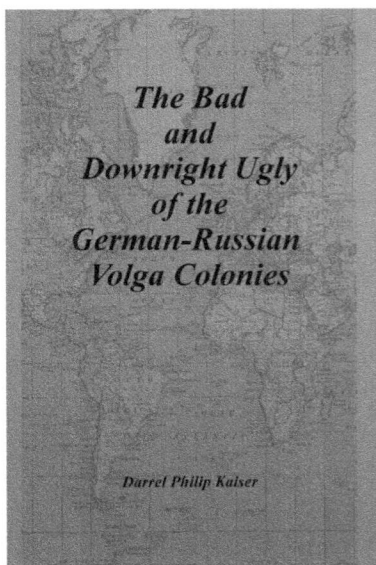

Origin & Ancestors
Families
Karle & Kaiser
of the
German-Russian Volga Colonies

Adolf	Heydmann	Rohr
Andreas	Hieronymus	Rudolph
Arp	Horn	Schaeffer
Arnst	Ekstadt	Scherer
Becker	Kaiser	Schiller
Bopp	Karle	Schmidt
Barbach	Köhler	Schmekler
Dagenheim	Krämer	Schütz
Fakt	Lieders	Simon
Freund	Maurer	Steitz
Gerlinger	Michel	Trieber
Grün	Neff	Trippel
Hari	Neumann	Vogt
Hellard	Nicolausen	Werner
Hermann	Nälmayer	Will
Hess	Popp	Zeichmann

Darrel Philip Kaiser

Moscow's
Final Solution:
The Genocide
of the
German-Russian
Volga Colonies

Darrel Philip Kaiser

Religions
of Germany
and the
German-Russian
Volga Colonies

Darrel Philip Kaiser

The Bad
and
Downright Ugly
of the
German-Russian
Volga Colonies

Darrel Philip Kaiser

Books by Darrel P. Kaiser
www.DarrelKaiserBooks.com

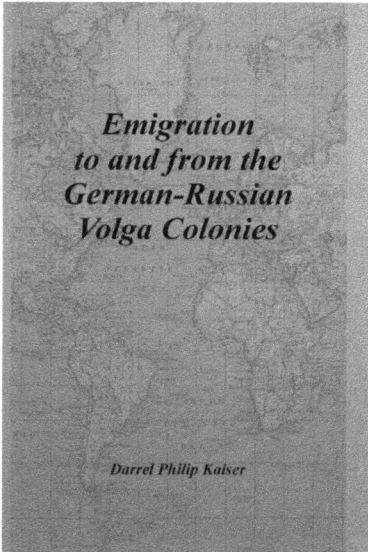

Emigration to and from the German-Russian Volga Colonies

Darrel Philip Kaiser

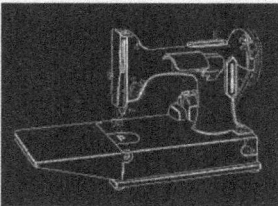

Basic Electrical Troubleshooting for Everyone

Darrel Philip Kaiser

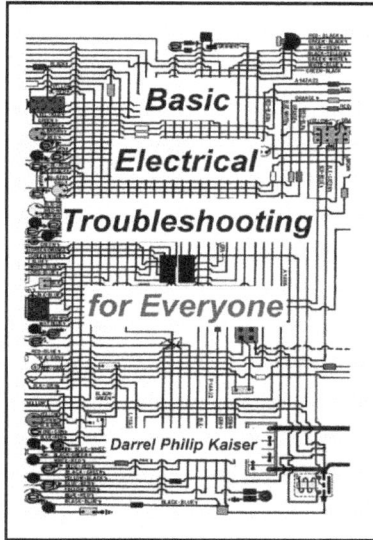

the Featherweight

Ads

Darrel P. Kaiser

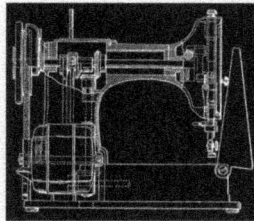

the Featherweight

Patents

Darrel P. Kaiser

Books by Darrel P. Kaiser
www.DarrelKaiserBooks.com

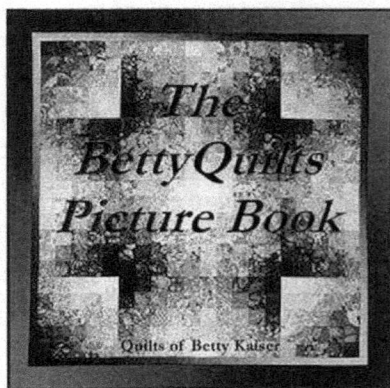

before the
Featherweight

Sewhandy
Volume 1
History

Darrel P. Kaiser

before the
Featherweight

Sewhandy
Volume 2
Maintenance
& Repair

Darrel P. Kaiser

**Logical
Sewing Machine
Troubleshooting**

ALL BRANDS

ANTIQUE - COMPUTER

for Everyone

Darrel Philip Kaiser

*The
BettyQuilts
Picture Book*

Quilts of Betty Kaiser

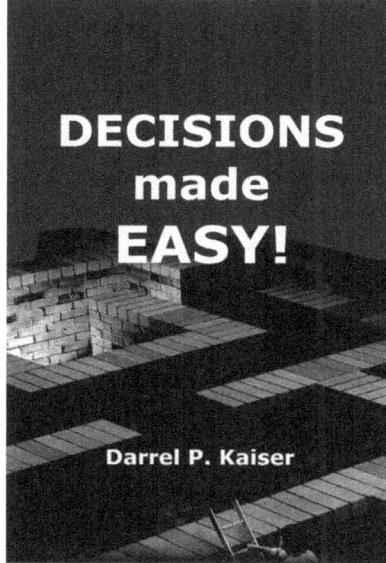

www.ingramcontent.com/pod-product-compliance
Lightning Source LLC
Chambersburg PA
CBHW030022290326
41934CB00005B/447